OF PERSONAL LIBERTY

the truth of motor vehicle infractions

Verl Engel

ISBN: 1508921334
ISBN 13: 9781508921332
Library of Congress Control Number: 2015904315
CreateSpace Independent Publishing Platform
North Charleston, South Carolina

Let us, then, with courage and confidence pursue our own Federal and Republican principles, our attachment to union and representative government...with all [our] blessings, what more is necessary to make us a happy and a prosperous people? Still one thing more, fellow-citizens—a wise and frugal Government, which shall restrain men from injuring one another, shall leave them otherwise free to regulate their own pursuits of industry and improvement, and shall not take from the mouth of labor the bread it has earned. This is the sum of good government, and this is necessary to close the circle of our felicities.

—Thomas Jefferson's first inaugural address

Each of us has a natural right—from God—to defend his person, his liberty, and his property. These are the three basic requirements of life, and the preservation of any one of them is completely dependent upon the preservation of the other two. For what are our faculties but the extension of our individuality? And what is property but an extension of our faculties? If every person has the right to defend even by force—his person, his liberty, and his property, then it follows that a group of men have the right to organize and support a common force to protect these rights constantly. Thus the principle of collective right—its reason for existing, its lawfulness—is based on individual right.

If this is true, then nothing can be more evident than this: The law is the organization of the natural right of lawful defense. It is the substitution of a common force for individual forces. And this common force is to do only what the individual forces have a natural and lawful right to do: to protect persons, liberties, and properties; to maintain the right of each, and to cause *justice* to reign over us all.

—Frédéric Bastiat, *The Law*

Acknowledgments

I want to acknowledge my friends Jason, John, and Brian for inspiring me to write this book. Without them, none of this would have been possible.

Special thanks to Hsuanwen Wang for helping me create the wonderful cover artwork.

Additional thanks to Danielle Jones and Devynn J. Payne for providing further help with the internal artwork and editing.

Lastly, I want to thank my parents for supporting me. Without their support, I would have never had the freedom necessary to realize my potential.

Table of Contents

Foreword

Imagine lights flash behind you, red and blue, and in the moment of surprise and incrimination, you begin to pull over. The officer in blue walks up after you dutifully stop, according to seemingly countless years of custom. She immediately inquires as to your velocity, seeking to use her aura of authority to back you into confessing to a perceived crime. You relinquish your documentation when impudently requested, and in return receive a citation obliging your remittance for a state-ordained wrongdoing.

What if you didn't have to stop? What if the law was actually on your side? The author of this book is going to convince you that this is the case. The Constitution of the United States of America is explicit in its limitations on governmental power and authority. You—as a citizen of the United

States of America—are the beneficiary of the trust that is the United States Constitution. The government—as the trustee—is forbidden from depriving people of their freedoms and unalienable rights without due process. Since the signing of the Constitution, the intervening centuries have quietly eroded the liberties of American citizens.

The government, particularly in the new millennium, has been accelerating this process of depriving Americans of liberties. The War on Terror has overseen the greatest of deprivations, from dismantling privacy of communications to banishing the right to a fair trial—rights guaranteed in the Constitution—all under the guise of necessity and security. The specter of an omniscient state divested of any trust in its citizens and void of any duty to protect their rights is not a distant nightmare. This is the waxing reality of the twenty-first-century police state. A reality often ignored by the average man or woman on the street, who lives happily in his or her fishbowl, always under the watchful eye of the government.

Our government, at this critical juncture, does not yet have full control of citizens' actions, but it seeks to corral people into ill-fitting but easily definable "safe" and "dangerous" categories. The following years will testify whether history turns this intrusive government into a tyrannical government or—if the people demand—into a government that deals respectfully and honestly with its beneficiaries.

Absolute power corrupts absolutely, and with the continuing consolidation of power in the hands of the government, the future of the United States of America as the land of the free is in jeopardy. The crux of the matter lies in how much the people are willing to concede before they stand up and say, "Enough." If the government can keep the apathetic populace adequately anesthetized to avoid questioning the accumulation of centralized power, then the transformation can continue undeterred. The government may then, and only then, fully take on the role of provider, controller, and dictator of not only what its citizens may not do, but also of what its citizens must do. This is the goal of a secure state, to dictate "good" behavior to its citizens and extirpate any residual resistance.

This book seeks to awaken people to the emergence of this totalitarian state. Will America return to being the land of the free, or will it manifest itself as the latest echo of authoritarian regimes proudly arrayed throughout history? As John Adams said, "Those who trade liberty for security deserve neither and lose both." Liberty depends on the responsibility of people to see and to act to thwart tyranny.

As one of "We the people," I humbly implore you not only to read this book but also to spend time comprehending its implications. As Thomas Jefferson said, "If a nation expects to be ignorant and free in a state of civilization, they expect what never was nor ever will be."

Andrew VanLoo
Vice President, Ravenheart Software, Ltd.

Preface

When I was a senior in college, I was pulled over by city police one night on my drive home. After I pulled my car to the side of the road, a police officer walked up to my window and gruffly demanded to see my license and registration, which I promptly provided. The officer then began to interrogate me: "Where are you going? How old are you? Do you have any weapons in the vehicle?" While this was happening, the officer's partner peered into the back windows of my car with his flashlight.

I knew that I had not been pulled over for speeding, nor could I think of anything else I had done wrong. Why, then, was the officer being so rough and giving me a shakedown? Despite the officer's uncordial nature, I answered all of his questions and focused on remaining polite.

After answering all of the officer's questions, I was then ordered to open my car's trunk. This really irked me; I could not understand why the officer would not take my word that I had nothing in the trunk. Alas, I complied with the officer's demand, as I was focusing solely on my desire to get home. When all was said and done, the officer gave me a verbal warning for a burned-out license plate light.

At the time, I was focused on affairs in school and did not pay much attention to the events of that evening. In hindsight, however, I felt violated. If the only problem the officer had with my driving was a burned-out license plate light, why didn't the officer simply tell me so and then let me go? Was there any *real* reason the officer felt the need to pry into my belongings, or was it simply standard operating procedure? This incident in my life ultimately inspired me to begin researching motor vehicle infractions so that I could be better prepared in the future.

What I have concluded from my research has astonished me. **I have reached five major conclusions**:

- Traveling on the public highways is a right and not a privilege

- Codes pertaining to motor vehicles do not pertain to the general public but only to people contractually using their automobiles for hire (e.g. taxis or semitrailers)

- Police must go through the process of getting a warrant before demanding that people show their identification or forfeit their belongings to a search

- The state can only enforce laws that directly relate to a distinct and palpable victim

- Courts routinely violate due process in order to obtain revenue from the infraction system

These conclusions highlight two significant philosophic problems in American society. First, they demonstrate that public education about rights enumerated in the Constitution has deteriorated; people are accustomed to blindly submitting to authority. Second, they show that the public has been subtly convinced—in error—that they do not own the highways.

The revenue generated from mandatory licensing, mandatory auto insurance, and enforcement of frivolous traffic tickets has turned administration of motor vehicle codes into a multibillion-dollar-a-year business—there is great profit in coercing the populace to, unknowingly, admit themselves as employed drivers.

Introduction

I wrote *Of Personal Liberty* to document my concerns pertaining to the administration of motor vehicle laws. Specifically, this book illustrates how government routinely violates law on many levels to acquire revenue for the state. I have arranged the subject matter as described below.

Chapters 1 and 2 focus on explaining why government was created and how it came to manifest. Did we break away from Britain simply to erect a new king, or was there a deeper philosophy as to how we ought to engage in governance with each other? How was our government structured? What checks and balances were established to ensure that government would be used the way that it was intended?

Chapters 3 and 4 focus on explaining how we are to understand written legislative law and, in turn, properly understand motor vehicle laws. How do we make sure that we understand a law correctly, and not merely interpret legislation any way we see fit? Do we have a proper understanding of motor vehicle laws, or are government officials leading us astray—unwittingly or otherwise?

Chapter 5 addresses the focal point of this book. If it is true that legislation does not require all motorized-travelers to get a driver's license, why would this be so? Is this merely a "legal loophole" that has been left unpatched, or is there a greater truth to uncover?

Chapters 6 and 7 focus on highlighting how government officials break the law in order to enforce motor vehicle infractions. What is the Fourth Amendment and how do police disrespect it by issuing traffic tickets? What laws, and notions of fair play, do the courts violate by ruling on traffic tickets?

Chapters 8 and 9 focus on confronting police and judicial powers. What are the best ways of interacting with police when they violate your rights? How should you appeal to a judge when you are putting forward arguments that they may not want to hear? What should you expect from all of this?

Ultimately, I have three GOALS for anyone who reads this book. First, readers should understand that we have a fundamental right to travel on the highways; the highways are owned and maintained by the public. Second, readers should prove appalled at the racketeering scheme resulting from police and judicial policy. Third, through discussing these issues, I hope to give readers a working knowledge of the maxims of law so that they can think critically about any political issue that may confront them.

1

Intent for Government

In order to understand the conclusions reached in the preface and meet the goals set in the introduction, we must first understand the intention behind the creation of the United States of America. **If you have not yet read the preface and introduction, please do so now before reading any further.**

COLONIAL HISTORY

First, it is necessary to understand the conditions under which the country was formed.

Prior to 1776, all of the people residing in the American colonies were subjects of the kingdom of Great Britain. At that time, the king of Great Britain was the sovereign[1] (monarch).

---

1 *Black's Law Dictionary*, 2d ed., s.v. "sovereign: A chief ruler with supreme power; a king or other ruler with limited power."

In other words, the government of Great Britain derived its powers from the decree of the king and the people had "civil rights" granted to them by the king.[2]

For a long period, the residents of the colonies (the soon to be states) were subjected to many abuses of power[3] from the King of Britain, including but not limited to:

U.S. Declaration of Independence (1776)

HE has dissolved Representative Houses repeatedly, for opposing with manly Firmness his Invasions on the Rights of the People.

...

HE has made Judges dependent on his Will alone, for the Tenure of their Offices, and the Amount and Payment of their Salaries.

...

HE has affected to render the Military independent of and superior to the Civil Power

...

HE has combined with others to subject us to a Jurisdiction foreign to our Constitution, and unacknowledged by our Laws; giving his Assent to their Acts of pretended Legislation:

...

FOR depriving us, in many Cases, of the Benefits of Trial by Jury:

---

2 Readers who wish to learn more are encouraged to research the Magna Carta.

3 The full list of offenses can be read in the Declaration of Independence.

This eventually led to the colonies' Declaration of Independence. When the colonies won the Revolutionary War in 1783, Britain was forced to acknowledge the colonies as sovereign.

Paris Peace Treaty (Peace Treaty of 1783), art. I
His Brittanic Majesty acknowledges the said United States, viz., New Hampshire, Massachusetts Bay, Rhode Island and Providence Plantations, Connecticut, New York, New Jersey, Pennsylvania, Delaware, Maryland, Virginia, North Carolina, South Carolina and Georgia, to be free sovereign and independent states, that he treats with them as such, and for himself, his heirs, and successors, relinquishes all claims to the government, propriety, and territorial rights of the same and every part thereof.

Once independence was declared, the equality of all men in right to life, liberty, and pursuit of happiness was acknowledged—**rights unalienable,** endowed in our state of nature, not subject to revocation by a government.[4] In other words, it was acknowledged that people have the right to use their natural inherent facilities as they see fit—insofar that no one else is harmed—prior to any obligations to human-made laws.[5] **Any**

---

4 Britain's government was known to revoke citizens' civil rights as a punishment for a crime—for instance, by declaring the person as not legally being allowed to own property or not having a right to a trial. Readers are encouraged to research the term *bill of attainder.*

5 The quotes from Thomas Jefferson and Fredrick Bastiat at the beginning of the book expand upon the idea of natural (unalienable) rights.

government, henceforth, was to be created by the people in order to secure individuals' unalienable rights.[6]

U.S. Declaration of Independence, paragraph 2 (1776)
WE hold these Truths to be self-evident, that **all Men are created equal,** that they are **endowed by their Creator with certain unalienable Rights,** that among these are Life, Liberty and the Pursuit of Happiness—That to secure these Rights, **Governments are instituted among Men, deriving their just Powers from the Consent of the Governed,** that whenever any Form of Government becomes destructive of these Ends, it is the Right of the People to alter or to abolish it, and to institute new Government, laying its Foundation on such Principles, and organizing its Powers in such Form, as to them shall seem most likely to effect their Safety and Happiness. (emphasis added)

To secure the unalienable rights acknowledged as a result of the Revolutionary War, many people desired to institute a federal Constitution. The federal Constitution was intended to be (and is) a charter[7] written to limit the powers of any government created within the United States.

---

6   For a better philosophic understanding of natural and unalienable rights, the reader is encouraged to read *The Law,* by Frederic Bastiat & *For a New Liberty The Libertarian Manifesto* by Murray N Rothbard.

7   *Black's Law Dictionary,* 2d ed., s.v. "charter: An instrument emanating from the sovereign power, in the nature of a grant, either to the whole nation, or to a class or portion of the people, or to a colony or dependency, and assuring to them certain rights, liberties, or powers. Such was the 'Great Charter' or 'Magna Charta,' and such also were the charters granted to certain of the English colonies in America. See Story, Const."

> The **constitution is a charter of negative liberties**; it tells the
> state to let the people alone; it does not require the federal gov-
> ernment or the states to provide services, even so elementary a
> service as maintaining law and order <u>Bowers v. Devito</u>, 686 F.2d 616
> (1982). (emphasis added)

> The rights and liberties which citizens of our country enjoy are not
> protected by custom and tradition alone, they have been jealously
> preserved from the encroachments of Government by express
> provisions of our written Constitution. <u>Reid v. Covert</u>, 354 U.S. 1, 1
> 1 L.Ed. 2d. 1148 (1957).

In attempts to persuade the people (of the original thirteen
states) to accept the proposal of a federal Constitution, three
of the founding fathers (Hamilton, Madison, and Jay) wrote a
series of detailed essays explaining what the proposed federal
Constitution would be. These essays are preserved in the book,
The Federalist Papers;[8] a book since ruled to be the exact record
of the intent of the framers of the United States Constitution.[9]

REPUBLICAN FORM OF GOVERNMENT

The founding fathers sought to institute a republican form
of government in hopes that it would secure individuals' unalienable rights.

---

8   Anyone who wishes to buy *The Federalist Papers: Hamilton, Madison, Jay* should
buy the Mentor unabridged edition.

9   <u>Cohens v. Virginia</u>, 19 U.S. 264 (1821). Many legal publications reference the
importance of *The Federalist Papers*.

When the founding fathers of the country drafted the U.S. Constitution, they intended to create a form of government that avoided monarchy. In addition, the founders desired to supersede a pure democracy; a government ruled solely by majority vote was liable to subject its citizens to mob rule.

That's not up for a vote.

By a faction, I understand a number of citizens, whether amounting to a majority or a minority of the whole, who are united and actuated by some common impulse of passion, or of interest, adversed to the rights of other citizens, or to the permanent and aggregate interests of the community...When a majority is included in a faction, the form of popular government [democracy], on the other hand, enables it [the faction] to sacrifice to its ruling passion or interest both the public good and the rights of other citizens. **To secure the public good and private rights against the danger of such a faction, and at the same time to preserve the spirit and the form of popular government [democracy], is then the great object to which our inquiries are directed.** (*The Federalist No. 10* at 78 (James Madison), (Clinton Rossiter ed., 1961); emphasis added)

The founding fathers understood that parts of government would need to be subject to popular vote for the public voice to be heard. However, the founders did not want any electoral process to have authority to oppress or override the unalienable rights of an individual. To accomplish this goal, the founders proposed (eventually instituted) government be administered as a *republic*.

> **A republic**, by which I mean a government in which the scheme of representation takes place, opens a different prospect, and **promises the cure for which we are seeking.** Let us examine the points in which it varies from pure democracy, and we shall comprehend both the nature of the cure and the efficacy which it must derive from the Union. [*Federalist No. 10* at 80 (James Madison), (Clinton Rossiter ed., 1961); emphasis added]

> **U.S. Const., article 4, § 4**
> The United States shall guarantee to every state in this union a **republican form of government**, and shall protect each of them against invasion; and on application of the legislature, or of the executive (when the legislature cannot be convened), against domestic violence. (emphasis added)

By a republic, the understanding was a form of government that would protect the unalienable rights of an individual against majorities (mobs) and other individuals. Pursuant to this goal, the republican form of government mandates that *all*[10] agents of government have their power derived from the people (via election) either directly or indirectly.[11]

> [W]e may define a republic to be, or at least may bestow that name on, a government which derives all its powers directly or in-directly from the great body of the people, and is administered by persons holding their offices during pleasure, for a limited period, or during good behavior...The House of Representatives, like that of one branch at least of all the State legislatures, is elected imme-diately by the great body of the people. The Senate, like the pres-ent Congress, and the Senate of Maryland, derives its appointment indirectly from the people. The President is indirectly derived from the choice of the people, according to the example in most of the States. Even the judges, with all other officers of the Union, will, as in the several States, be the choice, though a remote choice, of the people themselves. (*Federalist No. 39* at 241–242 (James Madison), (Clinton Rossiter ed.,1961))

> The first question that offers itself is, whether the general form and aspect of the government be strictly republican. It is evident that no other form would be reconcilable with the genius of the people of America; with the fundamental principles of the Revolution; or with that honorable determination which animates every votary

---

10 Both democratic and republican forms of government tend to use a *representational system* where citizens vote to elect politicians who represent their interests. However, our republican form of government has *all* of its agents derived from elections of the people; democratic forms of government may have agents that are independent from election of the people (e.g., queen of United Kingdom).

11 Federal Supreme Court justices (judges) are not directly elected by the people but instead are appointed into power by the president and legislators (Senate) as mandated in Article II, § 2 of the U.S. Constitution.

of freedom, to rest all our political experiments on the capacity of mankind for self-government. (*Federalist No. 39* at 240 (James Madison), (Clinton Rossiter ed.,1961))

The republican form of government was the only form of government that the founding fathers found adequate for their newly founded country.

CONSTITUTION IS A TRUST

On March 4, 1789, the charter known as the United States Constitution was instituted into law. To ensure that agents of government would work to secure individuals' unalienable rights, the charter was instituted in the form of a trust.[12]

Trusts are a special type of legal document—a written promise between individuals—that allows one person to become caretaker of an asset for another person.[13] The person who establishes the trust (typically the asset owner) is the Trustor, the person who will take care of the asset is the Trustee, and the person who will benefit from the caretaking is the beneficiary.

---

12 Some people would advocate that the Constitution is a contract instead of a trust. The problem with this view is that the Constitution does not impose any duties upon the people; it merely elicits how government is *trusted* to protect the people's unalienable rights. Furthermore, viewing the Constitution as a "social contract" implies that people are bound to a contract without having explicitly accepted or understood the terms in the contract.

13 *Black's Law Dictionary*, 5d ed., s.v. "Trust: A right of property, real or personal, held by one party for the benefit of another."

When someone becomes a trustee, he or she assumes *fiduciary duty*;[14] the trustee is obligated to prudently manage the asset in question for the sole benefit and interest of the beneficiaries.

Will you care for my property until my child inherits it?

Yes. I am bound by *fiduciary duty*.

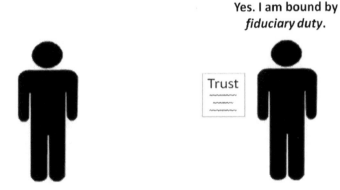

Trust

In many instances, trusts are written to safely allow a third party to manage an asset for an heir. For example, an asset owner (trustor) may write up a trust to allow a third party (trustee) to take care of a farm until their child (beneficiary) is old enough to inherit the property. Trusts can be written to manage any type of asset—property, money, or individuals' rights.

---

14 *Black's Law Dictionary,* 2d ed., s.v. "fiduciary: When one party must act for another. They are entrusted with the care of property or funds."

The U.S. Constitution was written as a trust—the founding fathers are the trustors, the government is the trustee, and the people are the beneficiaries.

> The delicacy and magnitude of *a trust* which so deeply concerns the political reputation and existence of every man engaged in the administration of public affairs, speak for themselves...The convention, it appears, thought the Senate the most fit depositary of **this important trust**. (*Federalist No. 65* at 397 (Alexander Hamilton), (Clinton Rossiter ed.,1961); emphasis added)

> The federal and State governments are in fact but different agents and **trustees of the people**, constituted with different powers, and designed for different purposes. (*Federalist No. 46* at 294 (James Madison), (Clinton Rossiter ed.,1961); emphasis added)

The parameters of the trust are outlined in the preamble of the Constitution:

> We the People of the United States, in Order to form a more perfect Union, establish Justice, insure domestic Tranquillity, provide for the common defense, promote the general Welfare, and secure the Blessings of Liberty to ourselves and our Posterity, do ordain and establish this Constitution for the United States of America

> **TRUSTOR**: We the People **[people of the original thirteen states]**
> **VENUE**: of the United States, **[country]**

PURPOSE: in Order to form a more perfect Union, establish Justice, insure domestic Tranquillity, provide for the common defense, promote the general Welfare, and secure
THE PROPERTY: the Blessings of Liberty **[unalienable individual rights]**
BENEFICIARY: to ourselves and our Posterity, **[future generations]**
ENABLING ACTION 1: do ordain **[declare the law]**
ENABLING ACTION 2: and establish **[bring into existence]**
WHAT: this Constitution **[articles of incorporation for trust]**
TRUSTEE: for the United States of America. **[government]**

In writing the Constitution as a trust, the people of the original thirteen states ensured that all government agents would be bound by fiduciary duty to serve the individuals of the public.[15] Government agents as trustees are obligated to manage the blessings of liberty (the asset) for the benefit of people (the beneficiaries).

> Constitutional provisions for the security of person and property are to be liberally construed, and "it is the duty of courts to be watchful for the constitutional rights of the citizen, and against any stealthy encroachments thereon." Byars v. U.S., 273 U.S. 28 (1927).

---

15   Many agents of government swear an oath to abide by the United States Constitution. See addendum 3.

Agents of government are required to administer the Constitution in a manner most *beneficial* to the individual (member of the people) who needs it at the time. In other words, government's protection of individuals' unalienable rights is preeminent to any philanthropic notion of common good; the **individual's rights come first**.[16]

---

16   The exception to this statement is when the country is at war, actively fighting an enemy off domestic soil. Certain liberties in that instance (such as soldiers dwelling in a private residence) are infringed upon to protect the homeland from an imminent threat.

2

Law in the United States

Now that we understand the intention for government's creation, we must now understand the significance of the U.S. Constitution and how laws in general are created.

SUPREME LAW OF THE LAND

The U.S. Constitution is the *supreme law of the land*; every government agent, law, and policy in the country must abide by this document.[17]

---

17 This was not true of the original 13 states at the founding of the United States. The original 13 states created the federal government and delegated certain powers to the federal government. However, since then, many states (e.g. Nevada) have declared themselves inferior to the U.S. Constitution or federal government. There are some states that have not declared themselves inferior to the U.S. Constitution or federal government, and theoretically could invoke nullification.

US Const. art. VI, cl. 2
This Constitution, and the laws of the United States which shall
be made in pursuance thereof; and all treaties made, or which shall
be made, under the authority of the United States, **shall be the
supreme law of the land**; and the judges in every state shall be
bound thereby, any-thing in the Constitution or laws of any State
to the contrary notwithstanding. (emphasis added)

The U.S. Constitution is a model that demonstrates the boundaries within which legitimate government conducts itself. The
Bill of Rights, in particular, exemplifies how government's
power is limited in order to respect the unalienable rights declared in the Declaration of Independence.

Besides the U.S. Constitution, there are also constitutions that
exist for each of the fifty states of America. A state's constitution is the supreme law for that state so long as the powers declared do not contradict the limitations of government
outlined in the U.S. Constitution. The U.S. Constitution and
states' constitutions serve as the outline for how our legal system is to be operated.

The people of the United States resident within any State are subject to two governments: one State, and the other National; but
there need be no conflict between the two. The powers which one
possesses, the other does not. United States v. Cruikshank, 92 U.S.
542 (1876).

DIVISION OF POWER

The U.S. Constitution mandates that the powers of government be separated into three branches: the legislative, executive, and judicial branches.[18]

The branches of government have the following roles:

- **The legislative** branch is responsible for embodying the *will* of the people in establishing order through the writing of law

- **The executive** branch is responsible for bringing *force* to law upon judicial mandate (or legislative declaration of war)

- **The judicial** branch is responsible to *judge* disputes in conformity with law so as to provide restitution

Paraphrasing, the authority of government is divided into will, force, and judgment. Authority is delegated to each branch in such a way so that power cannot be exercised unless all the branches cooperate. This division of power intends to prevent the oppression of the people and ensures that government should harmonize only towards the administration of justice.

---

18   This division of power can be seen in articles I–III of the U.S. Constitution.

We the People
of the United States, in Order to form a more
perfect Union, establish Justice, insure domestic
Tranquility, provide for the common defence,
promote the general Welfare, and secure the
Blessings of Liberty to ourselves and our
Posterity, do ordain and establish this Constitution
for the United States of America.

The U.S. Constitution

Legislative	Judicial	Executive
(Write Laws)	(Judge Laws)	(Enforce Laws)

ACTS OF LEGISLATORS

The U.S. Constitution mandates that the legislative branch be divided into two chambers and dictates how those chambers may use their power of *will* to create laws.

The legislative branch of government is made up of elected members of the public who are authorized to propose or sponsor laws on behalf of their fellow inhabitants. These legislators are divided into two chambers—the House and the Senate. Collectively, the House and the Senate are known as Congress.

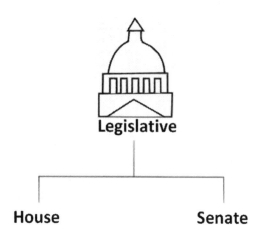

House   **Senate**

While any legislator can sponsor a bill (proposed law), bills can only successfully become law when approved by more than half the members of both the House and the Senate in addition to being approved by the executive branch; the president approves federal laws and the governor approves state laws. Alternatively, Congress can sanction a bill into law without the president/governor's approval by acquiring two-thirds support in both the House and Senate.

How Bills Become Law:

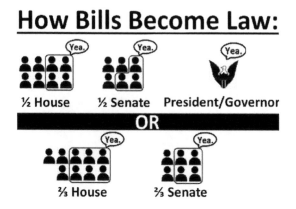

Once a bill is approved, it becomes a *statute*; this action is referred to as an "Act of Congress." Statutes are grouped with all the other statutes from the same legislative session (same year) to form a recorded volume titled *Statutes at Large* (federal laws) or *Session laws* (state laws). By tradition, though not the ideal, these volumes are codified by lawyers for ease of public reference. Specifically, the *codes* used to paraphrase the volumes are referred to as United States Code (U.S.C.)[19] and for Washington State, Revised Code of Washington (RCW),[20] respectively.[21] [22]

Because I (the author) live in Washington State, many examples in this book will use the RCW. However, because many states' codes are written and administered similarly, the examples given will still benefit those living in other states.

---

19   *United States Code* is maintained by the Office of the Law Revision Counsel (LRC) of the U.S. House of Representatives.

20   Washington State laws are codified by the Statute Law Committee and the Code Reviser.

21   Each state has a unique name for its own codes. For example, Washington State codes are referred to as RCW; Illinois codes are ILCS; North Carolina codes are NCGA, etc.

22   Many codes possess bracket citations at the bottom of the text in order to show the most recent statute the code is derived from. For example, the bottom of RCW 46.20.001 has the following bracketed citation: [1999 c 6 § 3.]. In this instance, the original statute can be traced back to the session laws of 1999, chapter 6, at section 3.

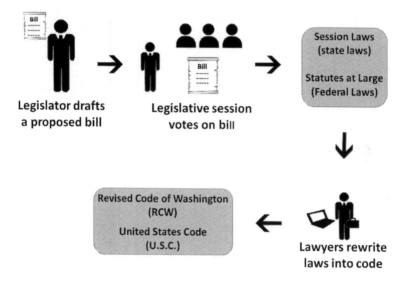

Legislator drafts
a proposed bill

Legislative session
votes on bill

Session Laws
(state laws)

Statutes at Large
(Federal Laws)

Revised Code of Washington
(RCW)

United States Code
(U.S.C.)

Lawyers rewrite
laws into code

3

Reading and Arguing Law

Now that we understand how laws are created, we shall discuss how to read and argue law.

READING LAW

Words used in everyday speech can mean very different things when used in law. For this reason, it's important to know how words in law are defined. There are two steps to defining words in law. The first is to see if statutes/session laws or codes define the word in question. If the word is not defined by statutes/session laws or codes, then a law dictionary should be used.

First: see if a word can be defined by the code.

Revised Codes of Wash. (RCW)

United States Code (U.S.C.)

Second: use a law dictionary to define words.

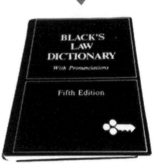

Step one: Statutes/Session laws are often poorly organized, making comprehension difficult. Oftentimes, it can be hard to understand terms or define words without reading the entire document. Although not the ideal, all laws are organized into codes and the codes are used for researching the definition of words.[23]

In order to research the definition of a word within the codes you must know that codes are organized into three parts: Titles >

---

23 Session laws or statutes may be necessary to reference if there is controversy with the code in question.

Chapters > Sections. Titles, much like the title of a book, specify the subject matter to be discussed; chapters break up the subject matter into categories, and the categories are made up of sections.

For example, let's assume we want to know how to define the word "vehicle" for a motor vehicle citation (traffic ticket) given in Washington State. To do this, we search within Title 46, *Motor Vehicles*, until we find the chapter for definitions; in the example illustrated above, it is chapter 4. Then we would search within that chapter until we find the section defining the term "vehicle"; in the example illustrated above, the section is 670.

Typically, every title contains a chapter designated for definitions. This chapter's purpose is to define words that, otherwise, may be unclear, controversial, or even contradictory to everyday speech. Readers must be diligent to ensure that they understand the word as it's defined in law, and consistently use that definition everywhere the word appears within a title.

Step two: If a word or term isn't defined within the law (codes) themselves, then definitions should be sought after in a law dictionary. Examples of accredited[24] law dictionaries that hold persuasive authority in court include *Bouvier's Law Dictionary* and *Black's Law Dictionary.*[25] Law dictionaries are unique from Standard English dictionaries in that they cite and excerpt Supreme Court cases to show how a term or idea was ruled to resolve a legal case.

ARGUING IN COMMON LAW

Now that we know how to define words within law, it is important to know how court arguments are typically formulated. To be successful at arguing law in court, it is necessary to show how higher courts in the past have ruled on legal disputes—that is, to cite *case law.*

Case law is referenced in order to identify, reiterate, or establish patterns of rulings; these patterns of rulings by higher courts are an authority known as *precedent.* Lower courts are required to respect precedent,[26] establishing a system of law referred to as *com-*

---

24 Any law dictionary used should be unabridged and printed by an accredited publisher, such as West Publishing.

25 Encyclopedias and other types of legal publications are discussed further in addendum 1.

26 In common law, originally, precedent was only referenced persuasively, judges were free to agree or disagree. At the turn of the 20th century, however, the policy of *Stare Decisis* has required that judges strictly adhere to previous higher court rulings. See addendum 5 for more information.

mon law.[27] The idea behind winning arguments in a common law legal system, such as we have in the U.S., is to cite higher court (ideally Supreme Court) case law in an attempt to **show precedent and thus mandate courts to rule in your favor.**[28]

To be able to use case law for legal battles, you need to be able to read legal citations. Legal citations allow you to enter a law library and navigate printed volumes, or search digitally using search engines such as Westlaw or LexisNexis.

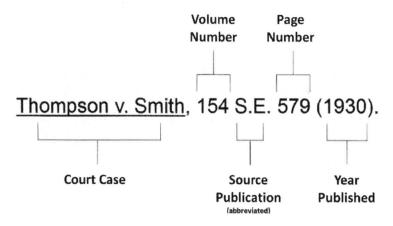

---

27 Court cases—precedent—can be overturned by new Supreme Court decisions or become invalidated by constitutional amendments.

28 *Stare Decisis*, the notion that precedent has a *mandatory* authority over lower court rulings, is not constitutional. Nonetheless, we shall learn how to argue law in accordance with Stare Decisis, as it is the standard operating procedure of everyone practicing law today. Stare Decisis is discussed in more detail in addendum 5.

For example, let's assume that we want to examine a particular case that discusses the right of citizens to travel on public highways. To do this, we would visit a law library and ask a librarian to help us find the published volumes that the court case is contained in; in the example illustrated above, it is the *South Eastern Reporter* (S.E.). Once found, we would then use the volume number to identify the specific book; in the example illustrated above, it is volume 154. Then we would turn to the appropriate page number; in the example illustrated above, it is page 579. Alternatively, law libraries have subscriptions to programs such as Westlaw or LexisNexis, allowing for the digital search of court cases by citation or key terms. [29]

Finding case law to support your legal arguments can be tricky; there is no silver bullet method. Case law can be found through word-of-mouth, key term search, law dictionaries,[30] and so on. You will have to play around in your research to find the court cases relevant to you.

Whenever possible, legal research should be done inside of a law library. While codes and case law can be located online, internet sources are not official and should only be used for self-reference purposes.

---

29 Virtually all of the case laws cited in this book have been vetted via Westlaw.

30 Law thesauruses and other resources for legal research are discussed further in addendum 1.

4

Examining Motor Vehicle Codes

When motor vehicle codes are examined carefully—all terms defined—it is discovered that they do not pertain to the majority of people traveling upon the highways. Contrary to popular belief, most people who travel upon public highways are not legally required to have a driver's license. Only people who use the roads to earn a wage are required to get a driver's license.

To illustrate, let's assume that you have been issued an infraction notice (ticket) for speeding in Washington State. The infraction notice will allege that you have violated the following law:

RCW 46.61.400
Basic rule and maximum limits.

(1) No person shall drive a vehicle on a highway at a speed greater than is reasonable and prudent under the conditions and having regard to the actual and potential hazards then existing. In every event speed shall be so controlled as may be necessary to avoid colliding with any person, vehicle or other conveyance on or entering the highway in compliance with legal requirements and the duty of all persons to use due care.

(2) Except when a special hazard exists that requires lower speed for compliance with subsection (1) of this section, the limits specified in this section or established as hereinafter authorized shall be maximum lawful speeds, and no person shall drive a vehicle on a highway at a speed in excess of such maximum limits.

    (a) Twenty-five miles per hour on city and town streets;

    (b) Fifty miles per hour on county roads;

    (c) Sixty miles per hour on state highways.

    The maximum speed limits set forth in this section may be altered as authorized in RCW 46.61.405, 46.61.410, and 46.61.415.

(3) The driver of every vehicle shall, consistent with the requirements of subsection (1) of this section, drive at an appropriate reduced speed when approaching and crossing an intersection or railway grade crossing, when approaching and going around a curve, when approaching a hill crest, when traveling upon any narrow or winding roadway, and when special hazard exists with respect to pedestrians or other traffic or by reason of weather or highway conditions.

This code seems self-evident; vehicles cannot exceed the speed limit on highways. However, it is important **not** to assume the meaning of any legal document without first putting due diligence into researching the terms in question. What exactly is a vehicle? Recalling the discussion in the previous chapter, definitions must first be sought after within the codes themselves.

RCW 46.04.670
Vehicle.
"Vehicle" includes every device capable of being moved upon a public highway and in, upon, or by which any persons or property is or may be **transported** or drawn upon a public highway, including bicycles. "Vehicle" does not include power wheelchairs or devices other than bicycles moved by human or animal power or used exclusively upon stationary rails or tracks. Mopeds are not considered vehicles or motor vehicles for the purposes of chapter 46.70 RCW. Bicycles are not considered vehicles for the purposes of chapter 46.12, 46.16A, or 46.70 RCW or RCW 82.12.045. Electric personal assistive mobility devices are not considered vehicles or motor vehicles for the purposes of chapter 46.12, 46.16A, 46.29, 46.37, or 46.70 RCW. A golf cart is not considered a vehicle, except for the purposes of chapter 46.61 RCW. (emphasis added)

A vehicle is defined as a device that moves upon the highway and may (is permitted to) *transport* things.[31] What is the definition of transportation?[32] Incidentally, transportation is not defined by code. Given that transportation is not defined by legislation, the next source for legal definitions would be precedents established in common law as cited in publications such as *Black's Law Dictionary*.[33]

> **Black's Law Dictionary, 2nd edition**
> **Transportation**
> The removal of goods or persons from one place to another, by a **carrier**. See Railroad Co. v. Pratt, 22 Wall. 133, 22 L.Ed. 827; Interstate Commerce Com'n v. Brimson, 154 U.S. 447, 14 Sup. Ct. 1125, 38 L.Ed. 1047; Gloucester Ferry Co. v. Pennsylvania, 114 U.S. 196, 5 Sup. Ct. 826, 29 L.Ed. 158. (emphasis added)

Transportation is defined as moving persons or goods by a *carrier*. Oddly, transportation is not simply defined as moving

---

31 Some states (e.g., California) omit the word *transport* from their definition of vehicle. It is important to read the original statute to see what the true definitions are. Regardless, most commonly used "motor vehicle" terms imply for hire. See appendix 1.

32 The word *drawn* is omitted from the discussion above because *drawn* is a reference to the use of a trailer. See: Act of Mar. 21, 1929, ch. 180 W.A. Laws 456 (An Act relating to vehicles and regulating the operations thereof upon the highways of this state).

33 When researching any legal term, it is important to make sure that the case law cited pre-dates the legislation (or contract) in question. In this example, the term *transportation* must be interpreted by case law pre-dating 1929 because those are the case laws that legislators at the time presumed when they first defined the term *vehicle* in statute. *Black's Law,* 2d ed., was published in 1910.

stuff, but explicitly as moving stuff with a carrier. What, then, is the definition of a carrier?[34]

> **Black's Law Dictionary, 2nd edition**
> **Common and Private Carriers**
> Carriers are either common or private. **Private carriers** are persons who undertake for the transportation in a particular instance only, not making it their vocation, **nor holding themselves out to** the public as ready to act for **all who desire their services**. Allen v. Sackrider, 37 N. Y. 341. To bring a person within the description of a **common carrier**, he must exercise it as a **public employment**; he must undertake to carry goods for persons generally; and he must hold himself out as **ready to transport goods for hire**, as a business, not as a casual occupation, *pro hac vice*. Alexander v. Greene, 7 Hill (N. Y.) 564; Bell v. Pidgeon, (D. C.) 5 Fed. 634; Wyatt v. Irr. Co., 1 Colo. App. 480, 29 Pac. 006. (*Black's Law Dictionary*, 2d ed.; emphasis added)

The definition of *private carrier* provided in Black's Law Dictionary 2nd edition is hard to read. To help clarify the definition, Black's Law Dictionary 5th edition is also referenced.

> **Black's Law Dictionary, 5th edition**
> **Carrier**
> Individual or organization engaged in transporting passengers or goods for hire.

---

34 The Black's Law Dictionary 2nd edition can be accessed online at thelawdictionary.org.

"Carrier" means any person engaged in the transportation of passengers or property by land, as a common, contract, or private carrier, or freight for-warder as those terms are used in the Interstate Commerce Act, and officers, agents and employees of such carriers. 18 U.S.C.A. § 831.

See also **Certified carriers; Connecting carrier; Contract carrier.**

Common carrier. Common carriers are those that hold themselves out or undertake to carry persons or goods of all persons indifferently, or of all who choose to employ it. Merchants Parcel Delivery v. Pennsylvania Public Utility Commission, 150 Pa.Super. 120, 28 A.2d 240, 244. Those whose occupation or business is transportation of persons or things for hire or reward. Common carriers of passengers are those that undertake to carry all persons indifferently who may apply for passage, so long as there is room, and there is no legal excuse for refusal.

Private carrier. Private carriers are those who transport only in particular instances and only for those they choose to contract with.

As it turns out, a carrier is someone who moves persons or goods on the highways for hire. In fact, the definition of motor vehicle in the federal code (Title 18 U.S.C. § 31) aligns with the definition discerned from state code.

18 U.S.C. § 31 : Definitions[35]

(6) Motor vehicle—The term "motor vehicle" means every description of carriage or other contrivance propelled or drawn by mechanical power and **used for commercial purposes** on the highways in the transportation of passengers, passengers and property, or property or cargo.

(10) Used for commercial purposes—The term "used for commercial purposes" means the carriage of persons or property for any fare, fee, rate, charge or other consideration, or directly or indirectly in connection with any business, or other undertaking intended for profit. (emphasis added)

When all the terms of interest have been legally defined, it is discovered that the term *vehicle* does not apply to all devices traveling on the road, but only devices[36] that are used *for hire*. [37] Legislators have no authority to license private travels on the

---

35   Title 18 of the U.S.C. provides definitions for criminal proceedings, which may cause skepticism given that infraction notices pertain to civil proceedings. Keep in mind, however, that if a person simply chooses to ignore motor vehicle laws (e.g., travel without a driver's license), he or she could be arrested, making the "motor vehicle" infraction criminal.

36   The term *automobile* is avoided to prevent any implication of being a vehicle. Many commonly used laymen terms are ultimately defined as *for hire*. See addendum 1 and appendix 1.

37   The first motor vehicle statute that required registering/licensing "motor vehicles" was in 1915. The definition of "public highway" within this statute makes a clear distinction between "transportation" and "travel." See Act of March 17, 1915, Ch. 142 W.A. Laws 386 (An Act relating to the use of the public highways).

public highways.[38] Any alleged jurisdiction to enforce these codes on non-for-hire travel is subject to demurrer.[39]

This is not a legal loophole to avoid compliance with motor vehicle laws. It cannot be assumed that legislators were ambiguous in their use of terminology. The correct interpretation of motor vehicle laws lays at the heart of *personal liberty* as historically established in common law.[40]

> The right of the citizen to travel upon the highway and to transport his property thereon, in the ordinary course of life and business, differs radically and obviously from that of one who makes the highway his place of business for private gain... State v. City of Spokane, 186 P. 864 (1920).

> It is intended to apply to "for hire" vehicles as distinguished from auto stages. "For hire" vehicles...are defined to mean all motor vehicles other than automobile stages used for the transportation of persons for which transportation remuneration of any kind is received, either directly or indirectly. International Motor Transit Co. v. Seattle, 251 P. 120. (1926).

38　See also: Act of March 9, 1933, Ch. 166 W.A. Laws 613 (An Act relating to transportation by motor vehicles).

39　*Black's Law,* 2d ed., s.v. "demurrer: … an allegation that, even if the facts as stated in the pleading to which objection is taken to be true, yet their legal consciences are not such as to put the demurring party to the necessity of answering them or proceeding further with the cause."

40　See also: addenda 2–4.

Discussion of commercial driver's licenses and *for hire vehicles* is provided in Addendum 2.

5

Personal Liberty

The highways are owned and maintained by the people as a means of expressing personal liberty; private travel upon the highways is a right that cannot be deprived through licensing. Extraordinary uses of the highways, such as using the highways as a medium for conducting business, are subject to licensing.

INDIVIDUAL RIGHTS

Personal liberty is a feature of liberty generally, referring specifically to the freedom of people to move about, unencumbered, of their own will.

> **Black's Law Dictionary, 5th edition**
> **Personal liberty.**
> The right or power of locomotion; of changing situation, or moving one's person to whatsoever place one's own inclination may

direct, without imprisonment or restraint, unless by due course of law.

Included in personal liberty is the right to travel in a motorized device on the public highways[41] within and between the states freely. Highways are created and publicly funded by people in order to express personal liberty.[42] People appointed a government as a caretaker (trustee) for the highways that are owned by the public.

> Undoubtedly the right of locomotion, **the right to remove from one place to another according to inclination, is an attribute of personal liberty**, and the right, ordinarily, of **free transit** from or through the territory of any state **is a right secured** by the Fourteenth Amendment and by other provisions of the Constitution. <u>Williams v. Fears</u>, 343 U.S. 270, 274. (1900). (emphasis added)

> The streets of the cities of this country belong to the public. Primarily, every member of the public has the ***natural right* to the free use of such streets** in the normal pursuit of his private or personal business or pleasure. In his errands of pleasure, he may use these highways to his heart's content...**These rights, being inherent in him as an American citizen, cannot be taken away**

41 In the 1960's the term *public highway* was defined as "[E]very way or place in the state open as a matter of right to public vehicular travel." The agenda to refer to travel as a privilege instead of a right is relatively new. See: Act of Feb. 27, 1959, Ch. 49 W.A. Laws 413 (An Act relating to motor vehicles).

42 See appendix 2

from him, or unreasonably restricted or regulated. Subject to this freedom of personal conduct inherent in the individual, however, the control of the streets of the cities rests in the Legislature, **acting as trustee for the public.** The right of the public at large to the free use of the streets is paramount to the natural right of the individual, and the Legislature, in its capacity as trustee, has the power to reasonably regulate this use, to the end that the public shall enjoy the maximum benefits thereof. <u>City of San Antonio v. Fetzer</u>, 241 S.W. 1034 (1922). (emphasis added)

Some courts have ruled (since the passing of motor vehicle legislation) that government may subject people to permitting or licensing in attempts to ensure safe use of public highways. Simultaneously, the courts assert that travel on the public highways is the peoples' natural/unalienable right.

The regulation of the exercise of the right to drive a private automobile on the streets of the city may be accomplished in part by the city by granting, refusing, and revoking, under rules of general application, permits to drive an automobile on its streets; but such permits may not be arbitrarily refused or revoked, or permitted to be held by some and refused to other of like qualifications, under like circumstances and conditions. <u>Thompson v. Smith</u>, 154 S.E. 579 (1930).

The right of a citizen to travel upon the public highways and to transport his property thereon in the ordinary course of life and business is a common right which he has under **his right to enjoy life and liberty**, to acquire and possess property, **and to pursue happiness and safety**. It includes the right in so doing to use the

> ordinary and usual conveyances of the day; and under the existing modes of travel includes the right to drive a horse-drawn carriage or wagon thereon, or to operate an automobile thereon, for the usual and ordinary purposes of life and business. Thompson v. Smith, 154 S.E. 579 (1930). (emphasis added)

This is a judicial error. It is nonsense to assert that individuals have the right to travel upon the highways, but only after they first ask for permission (acquire a permit/license)[43] to exercise that right. The highways are inherently owned by the public: individuals of the public don't need to ask for anyone's permission to be allowed to travel upon the highways.

> The streets and highways belong to the public. They are built and maintained at public expense for the use of the general public in the ordinary and customary manner. Hadfield v. Lundin, 98 Wash 516. (1917).

It is contradictory for courts to imply that people have an innate, natural, *unalienable*,[44] right to travel upon public highways only after being granted permission (a license) by the government. If someone is forced to meet government prerequisites (e.g. licensing) before being allowed to travel, then that individual is necessarily

---

43 *Black's Law Dictionary*, 5th ed., s.v. "license: The permission by competent authority to do an act which, without such permission, would be illegal, a trespass, or a tort. People v. Henderson, 391 Mich. 612, 218 N.W.2d 2, 4."

44 While Thompson v. Smith does not explicitly use the phrase *unalienable*, its meaning is readily implied in reference to "life, liberty, and pursuit of happiness"—unalienable rights mentioned in the Declaration of Independence.

alienated/deprived of their liberty to travel until their conduct is sanctioned by government approval: this is unconstitutional.

Did you get permission to use these highways?

Why do I need permission to travel?

Am I not assumed innocent (able) to drive until proven otherwise?

Any deprivations of a person's liberty must be done with a cause and with due process of law. [45]

U.S. Const. amend. V

No person shall be held to answer for a capital, or otherwise infamous crime, unless on a presentment or indictment of a Grand Jury, except in cases arising in the land or naval forces, or in the Militia, when in actual service in time of War or public danger; nor shall any person be subject for the same offense to be twice put in jeopardy of life or limb; nor shall be compelled in any criminal case to be a witness against himself, **nor be deprived of life, liberty, or property, without due process of law;** nor shall private property

---

45 "The essential elements of due process of law are...notice and the opportunity to defend" <u>Simon v. Craft</u>, 182 U.S. 427.

be taken for public use, without just compensation. (emphasis
added)

Specifically, people cannot be denied, preemptively or otherwise, the liberty to exercise their right to travel unless they
have heard a charge (complaint) brought against them and
are given an opportunity to defend themselves (answer) in
court.

> To be that statute which would deprive a Citizen of the **rights
> of person or property**, without a regular trial, according to the
> course and usage of the common law, would not be the law of the
> land. Hoke v. Henderson, 15 N.C. 15. (emphasis added)

> The right to travel is a part of the 'liberty' of which the citizen can-
> not be deprived without the due process of law under the Fifth
> Amendment. So much is conceded by the Solicitor General. In
> Anglo-Saxon law that right was emerging at least as early as the
> Magna Carta. Kent v. Dulles, 357 U.S. 116 (1958).

If an individual's liberty to exercise a right is converted into a
privilege, that person ought to, in theory, be able to ignore the
licensing without fear of punishment.

> And our decisions have made clear that a person faced with such
> an unconstitutional licensing law may ignore it and engage with
> impunity in the exercise of the right of free expression for which

the law purports to require a license. <u>Shuttlesworth v. Birmingham</u>, 394 U.S. 147. (1969).

Personal liberty—any liberty—cannot be arbitrarily deprived from the public.

> The fourteenth amendment, in declaring that no state "shall deprive any person of life, liberty, or property without due process of law, nor deny to any person within its jurisdiction the equal protection of the laws," undoubtedly intended not only that there should be no arbitrary deprivation of life or liberty... <u>Barbier v. Connolly</u>, 113 U.S. 27, 31. (1884).

An individual's right to personal liberty is an unalienable right that government needs to respect.

PUBLIC RIGHTS

While personal liberty is a right that cannot be *deprived* through licensing, it can be *regulated* when exercised on public highways.

As aforementioned, if an individual has the right to do something, they cannot be required to register with the state (get a license) before being allowed to do that thing. Insofar that individuals' have the right to travel upon the highways, they cannot be required to get a driver's license as a condition to being granted access to the highways.

However, because all individuals of the public commonly own the highways, people necessarily share their right to travel upon the highways with others; the individual's right becomes a public right. Public rights, while exempt from deprivation (licensing), may be subject to regulations (rules of the road) to ensure safe and equitable access to the highways. In other words, individuals cannot be required to get a driver's license before being allowed to travel upon the highways, but they can be held liable if they harm someone else in violating the 'assumed and presumed' rules of the road (e.g. not stopping at a red light).

> They all recognize...**the ordinary Right of the Citizen to use the streets in the usual way**... **the legislative power is confined to regulation**... Hadfield v. Lundin, 98 Wash 516 (1917). (emphasis added)

> The right of a citizen to travel upon the public highways and to transport his property thereon in the ordinary course of life and business is a common right which he has under his right to enjoy life and liberty..." The rights aforesaid, being fundamental, are constitutional rights, and while the exercise thereof **may be reasonably regulated** by legislative act in pursuance of the police power of the State, and although those powers are broad, **they do not rise above those privileges which are imbedded in the constitutional structure.** The police power cannot justify the enactment of any law which amounts to an arbitrary and unwarranted interference with, or unreasonable restriction on, those

rights of the citizen which are fundamental. State v. Armstead, 103 Miss. 790, 799, 60 So. 778, Ann. Cas.1915B, 495." <u>Teche Lines, Inc., v. Danforth,</u>12 So.2d 784 (1943). (emphasis added)

While all individuals have the right to travel on public highways for their own leisure, the judicial branch has ruled that people do not have the right to bogart the highways as a medium for conducting business.[46] People who are "on the clock" (for hire) when they drive have to acquire special permission—a license—to use public highways. Insofar as drivers are licensed, they are subject to the restrictions of a license; licensed drivers must comply with motor vehicle codes.

They all recognize the **fundamental distinction between the ordinary Right of the Citizen to use the streets in the usual way and the use of the streets as a place of business** or a main instrumentality of business for private gain. The former is a common Right, the latter is an extraordinary use. **As to the former, the legislative power is** *confined to regulation,* **as to the latter, it is plenary and extends even to absolute prohibition.** Since the use of the streets by a common carrier in the prosecution of its business as such is not a right but a mere license of privilege. <u>Hadfield v. Lundin</u>, 98 Wash 516 (1917). (emphasis added)

---

46   To use an analogy, while all tenants in a house are entitled to the use of the kitchen, if one tenant wants to use the house's kitchen to host a bake sale, then that tenant ought to acquire permission from the other tenants before he or she bogarts the common space. In this case, people using highways for personal revenue must license themselves to the caretaker (trustee) of the highways—the government.

First, it is well established law that the highways of the state are public property, and their primary and preferred use is for private purposes, and that their use for purposes of gain is special and extraordinary which, generally at least, the legislature may prohibit or condition as it sees fit. Stephenson v. Rinford, 287 U.S. 251 (1932).

You can't use the highways to make money without getting permission first!

The unfortunate nature of today's society is that our government no longer distinguishes between those who are traveling upon the highways by privilege (for hire) and those that are traveling by right (personal liberty). Government indiscriminately requires everyone to acquire a driver's license in lieu of civil penalties or arrest.

Where rights secured by the Constitution are involved, there can be no rule [policy] making or legislation which would abrogate [deprive] them. Miranda v. Arizona, 384 U.S. 436 (1966).

We find it intolerable that one Constitutional Right should have to be surrendered in order to assert another. <u>Simons v. United States</u>, 390 U.S. 389 (1968).

It is wrong for the state and municipalities (cities) to require everyone to have a driver's license before being allowed to travel upon the highways. Motor vehicle codes, as they are currently administered, cannot be sanctioned by law and must be exposed as oppressive in nature.

6

Fourth Amendment Violations

Contrary to public policy, law enforcement's unwarranted demands for personal "papers" (driver's license, vehicle registration, and proof of auto insurance) are unlawful and disrespectful to individuals' rights.

INTENTION OF THE FOURTH AMENDMENT

The Fourth Amendment is an amendment in the U.S. Constitution (Bill of Rights) stipulating when and how government authorities may forcefully confiscate and examine individuals or their belongings. To understand the ramifications of the Fourth Amendment, it is important to understand colonial history before the American Revolutionary War.

When the American colonies were subject to English customs, it was not uncommon for citizens to feel violated by random searches of their homes from police officials. Specifically, customs officers could acquire what was called a *writ of assistance*—a general document that gave officers authority to enter premises, using force if necessary, to search for any materials or documents indicating that goods were being imported illegally.

A writ of assistance functioned much like search warrants do today, except that it did not specify the place to be searched and was valid for an unlimited time. In effect, custom officers had blanket authority to search (harass) citizens whenever they desired. Ultimately, any form of *general* warrant was prohibited by the Virginia Declaration of Rights[47] and in turn the Fourth Amendment to the Constitution of the United States.[48]

Virginia Declaration of Rights, Section 10
That general warrants, whereby an officer or messenger may be commanded to search suspected places without evidence of a fact committed, or to seize any person or persons not named, or whose offense is not particularly described and supported by evidence, are grievous and oppressive and ought not to be granted.

---

47 The Fourth Amendment is said to have been derived from the Virginia Declaration of Rights (section 10).

48 A full list of oppressions by the king of Great Britain can be read in the Declaration of Independence of the United States of America.

U.S. Const. amend. IV
The right of people to be secure in their persons, houses, papers, and effects, against unreasonable searches and seizures shall not be violated, and no Warrants shall issue, but upon probable cause, supported by Oath or affirmation, and particularly describing the place to be searched, and the persons or things to be seized.

The requirement of a *specific* warrant for people to forfeit *any* papers or belongings to search by police powers was an intentional safeguard established by the founding fathers. Specifically, the requirement of an officer to swear an oath or otherwise affirm that probable cause exists protects people from frivolous searches/seizures and proceedings. If a judge grants a warrant based on an oath or affirmation that is later found to be falsified, that officer can be held liable.

Please grant me a warrant! I swear to be telling the truth.

Granted.

The purpose for specific warrants—particularly describing the things to be searched for or seized—is to ensure that there is a hassle and liability associated with infringing on peoples' rights; stringent laws safeguard against police powers who would impose themselves on people for frivolous or malicious reasons. Police powers cannot have jurisdiction to search a person's papers or belongings through *any form* of a general warrant (legislative or judicial sanction) [49] without compromising the integrity of the Fourth Amendment. Any sanctioning of an officer's demand to search papers or belongings without a *specific* warrant is explicitly unconstitutional.

UNWARRANTED SEARCHES

Despite objections, some courts have ruled that automobiles' papers are exempt from the requirement of a search warrant.

The first case law cited for permitting police powers to search an automobile without a warrant was <u>Carroll v. United States</u> in 1925. In this particular case, judges ruled that police had authority to search an automobile without a warrant on suspicion that the vehicle may be carrying contraband (alcohol).

---

49   It does not matter if an alleged sanctioning is established from statutes (legislators) or through case law (judges): any search *generally* through a person's things, without a specific warrant is acting contrary to the intent of the Fourth Amendment.

The presiding judges felt that the automobile searches were not a violation of the Fourth Amendment.

> The conference report resulted, so far as the difference between the two houses was concerned, in providing for the punishment of any officer, agent, or employee of the government who searches a "private dwelling" without a warrant, and for the punishment of any such officer, etc., who searches any "other building or property" where, and only where, he makes the search without a warrant "maliciously and without probable cause." In other words, it left the way open for searching an automobile or vehicle of transportation without a warrant, if the search was not malicious or without probable cause.
>
> The intent of Congress to make a distinction between the necessity for a search warrant in the searching of private dwellings and in that of automobiles and other road vehicles in the enforcement of the Prohibition Act is thus clearly established by the legislative history of the Stanley Amendment. **Is such a distinction consistent with the Fourth Amendment? We think that it is, The Fourth Amendment does not denounce all searches or seizures, but only such as are unreasonable**. Carroll v. United States, 267 U.S. 132 (1925). (emphasis added)

The precedent set in Carroll v. United States is fallacious for a few reasons:

- Judicial sanctioning of warrantless searches is not an administration of the Constitution most favorable for the *beneficiary;* the judges opted to violate the individual's right to a warranted search to make admitting evidence easier.[50]

- Any sanctioning of police searches without a specific warrant from a judge is a violation of the Constitution's delegations of power; the judiciary is the only branch of government with authority to *judge* if a particular search is reasonable.[51]

- This precedent exempting warranted searches should have no applicability on private citizens; it utilizes terminologies that are defined as *for hire* travel.[52]

Since <u>Carroll v. United States</u>, many precedents have been established that permit the searching of a vehicle's papers without a warrant. In general, proponents have argued that if police wait to obtain a warrant before they can search a device as mobile as an automobile, the time delay could jeopardize the police officers attempt to discover incriminating evidence. However, many of the delays that occurred in the 1920s have been offset by 21st century technological advancements—not

---

50 See chapter: "Intent for Government".

51 See chapter: "Law in the United States"

52 Individuals who utilize the public highways as mediums for business are considered to be engaged in public affairs and therefore (allegedly) exempt from protection by the Fourth Amendment. See chapter "Personal Liberty."

that any excuse should allow government agents to prioritize evidence gathering over people's rights.

Despite the aforementioned contentions, government will continue to perpetuate unwarranted vehicle searches until there is a new groundbreaking precedent or social reform. Instead, the more practicable objection to make is that police powers lack a genuine *reason* to search a person's papers; this can be demonstrated even if the motor vehicle laws are acquiesced into.

UNREASONED SEARCHES

Even if people are using the highways *for hire*, committing an infraction is not sufficient grounds to demand an employed person's papers.

When police powers detain[53] people for committing motor vehicle infractions, people assume their first step is to provide the police officer with their papers when requested. There are motor vehicle codes that say if people do not provide an officer with the documentation asked for upon *demand*, they are guilty of a misdemeanor, guilty of breaking a law.

---

53   The reader is encouraged to research the legal term *Terry stop* for clarification of this idea.

RCW 46.61.020

Refusal to give information to or cooperate with officer—Penalty. (1) It is unlawful for any person while operating or in charge of any vehicle to refuse when **requested** by a police officer to give his or her name and address and the name and address of the owner of such vehicle, or for such person to give a false name and address, and it is likewise unlawful for any such person to refuse or neglect to stop when signaled to stop by any police officer or to refuse upon **demand** of such police officer to produce his or her certificate of license registration of such vehicle, his or her insurance identification card, or his or her vehicle driver's license or to refuse to permit such officer to take any such license, card, or certificate for the purpose of examination thereof or to refuse to permit the examination of any equipment of such vehicle or the weighing of such vehicle or to refuse or neglect to produce the certificate of license registration of such vehicle, insurance card, or his or her vehicle driver's license when requested by any court. Any police officer shall on request produce evidence of his or her authorization as such. (emphasis added)

However, upon close inspection, the code cited for jurisdiction makes a clear distinction between a legal *demand* and a *request*. A request is merely when an individual asks someone for something; a demand is when an authority forces a person to comply with a request under jurisdiction of law.

Black's Law Dictionary, 5th ed
Request
An asking or petition; the expression of a desire to some person for something to be granted or done.

Black's Law Dictionary, 2d ed.
Legal demand
A demand properly made, as to form, time, and place, by a person lawfully authorized.

In order for a citing officer to have the jurisdiction of law to force an infractor's papers to be revealed, the officer's actions must be in accordance with his or her fiduciary duty implied by the Constitution. Specifically, even *if* an officer had authority to search a motor vehicle without a warrant, the officer still must provide a reason as to why he or she believes examination of a person's belongings was *necessary*. In other words, an officer's search of papers is *unreasonable* if the officer's job could be completed without acquiring the infractor's papers.[54]

In accordance with the Revised Codes of Washington (RCW), it is not necessary for an officer to acquire a driver's papers to issue an infraction notice. A citing officer (albeit to his or her inconvenience) could document the name

---

54 Recall in the chapter "Intent for Government" that all agents of government are trustees of the people. Police powers, as a matter of duty, must do anything they can to avoid any unnecessary infringements of individual's rights enumerated in the Constitution.

and address verbally provided to them and then record the make, model, and license plate number of the car; an officer can mail a copy of the citation to the vehicle's registered address.[55] Given that an officer can acquire all of the necessary information to issue an infraction notice without demanding papers, any demand for papers would clearly be an excessive use of force and consequentially a violation of the Fourth Amendment.[56]

Moreover, detaining someone for committing a motor vehicle infraction does not alone establish a reason to search that person's papers for further illegal activity. There is no logical reason to believe that just because a person committed an infraction (e.g., speeding), he or she also possesses a stolen vehicle or suspended license/insurance: the only crimes directly discoverable by those papers. If an officer cannot articulate an *explicit* reason why searching a person's papers will more likely than not reveal a crime—probable cause—then the search is necessarily *unreasoned* and therefore *unreasonable*.

---

55 Police could document what they saw, get a warrant, and then access the driver's registration information to issue an infraction. Persons using the highways for hire would presumably have their vehicles registered with the government; persons traveling by right (and not by privilege) would not be registered with the government and would, in practice, not be subject to traffic tickets.

56 If someone is committing more than an infraction, if they are recklessly driving or otherwise pose an immediate threat to others, they may be arrested until matters can be resolved.

**I caught you speeding!
Let me see your papers.**

**Searching my papers wont help you
prove that I was speeding. Why do
you need to see my papers?**

It may then be asked: if an officer cannot acquire papers under most circumstances, how then would an officer ensure that an infractor has a valid license and auto insurance? The appropriate response is that officers are not allowed to conduct haphazard searches but only searches supported by probable cause. Conducting unreasoned searches of people for compliance to the law is explicitly against the spirit of the Fourth Amendment of the Constitution.

Alas, police powers violate peoples' Fourth Amendment rights at virtually all traffic stops conducted. However, lawfully, people should not be punished for defending their unalienable rights enumerated in the Constitution:

> [It is of] obvious concern that there be no sanction or penalty imposed upon one because of his exercise of constitutional rights. Sherar v. Cullen, 481 F. 946 (1973).

...[T]he assertion of federal rights, when plainly and reasonably made, is not to be defeated under the name of local practice. Davis v. Wechsler, 263 US 22, at 24 (1923).

Probable cause is not established by failing to present identification upon request by a law enforcement officer. Moya v. United States, 761 F.2d 322, at 325-326 (1984).

The Texas statute under which appellant was stopped and required to identify himself is designed to advance a weighty social objective in large metropolitan centers: prevention of crime. But even assuming that purpose is served to some degree by stopping and demanding identification from an individual without any specific basis for believing he is involved in criminal activity, the guarantees of the Fourth Amendment do not allow it. Brown v. Texas, 443 U.S. 47, (1979).

Here, by contrast, the defendants simply refused to produce identification other than the airline tickets. If the Georgia statute were construed to require, not only truthful identification, but proof of truthfulness on demand, it would be unconstitutional. See *Kolender v. Lawson*, 461 U.S. 352, 103 S.Ct. 1855, 1859–60, 75 L.Ed.2d 903 (1983). We therefore must interpret the statute to prohibit only actual lies in order to avoid an unconstitutional construction. The defendants' refusal to furnish identification—which they were entitled to do if indeed this was a *Terry* stop, as the government must contend—may have created suspicion that they had actually used false names, but falls far short of probable cause. Of course, when Manikowski's wallet was seized and was found to contain identification conflicting with his ticket, probable cause was established;

but this occurred only after the seizure and therefore cannot be used to justify it. <u>U.S. v. Brown</u>, 731 F.2d 1491, at 1494 (1984).

The rights and liberties which citizens of our country enjoy are not protected by custom and tradition alone, they have been jealously preserved from the encroachments of Government by express provisions of our written Constitution. <u>Reid v. Covert</u>, 354 U.S. 1 at 1 L.Ed. 2d. 1148 (1957).

People are persuaded into forfeiting constitutional rights for a few reasons:

- People are ignorant about the Constitution and its legal significance to themselves and the law.

- People are ignorant as to the meaning and scope of the codes that police powers cite to assume jurisdiction.

- People who do not defend their constitutional rights in a timely manner have their right to complain expire; the legal concept "laches"[57] takes effect.

---

57 *Black's Law Dictionary*, 2nd ed., s.v. "laches: Negligence, consisting in the omission of something which a party might do, and might reasonably be expected to do, towards the vindication or enforcement of his rights."

7

Hypocrisy of Infraction Courts

It has been shown that motor vehicle laws are being misapplied to non-employed travelers in violation of their constitutional rights. What will now be shown is that the process by which infraction notices are tried in Washington State courts is a contradiction of law.

THE STATE HAS NO STANDING

Ultimately, the state has no authority to file lawsuits (traffic tickets) against people because the state cannot prove that any person's rights were infringed upon or harmed.

Within the Washington State Constitution, it is said that the intent (purpose) of government is to protect and maintain individual rights.[58]

Wash. Const. art. I, § 1
All political power is inherent in the people, and governments derive their just powers from the consent of the governed, and are established to protect and maintain individual rights.

If a person commits an act of kidnapping or murder, that person deprives another individual of their right to liberty or life respectively—rights unalienable, acknowledged by the Declaration of Independence and enumerated by the constitutions. Creating and enforcing laws prohibiting such behavior is a protection of peoples' individual rights. Any law created or enforced that does not functionally protect and maintain individuals' rights is not authorized by the constitution and is outside the intent for government.

Speeding tickets and all infraction notices are claimed to be civil proceedings by Washington State courts. In other words, infractions are not criminal offenses but civil cases; people are

---

58　Most state constitutions mention that people have unalienable rights, but few constitutions state as explicitly as the Washington Constitution that government is to protect *individual rights*. However, protection of individual rights is mandated in the Declaration of Independence. See chapter: "Intent for Government".

having *lawsuits* filed against them by the state (or city) for committing an infraction.

> IRLJ
> Rule 1.2
> DEFINITIONS
>
> For the purposes of these rules:
>
> (a) Infraction Case. **"Infraction case" means a civil proceeding** initiated in a court of limited jurisdiction pursuant to a statute that authorizes offenses to be punished as infractions.
>
> (b) Notice of Infraction. **"Notice of infraction" means a document initiating an infraction case** when issued and filed pursuant to statute and these rules. (emphasis added)

However, a plaintiff cannot possess standing to file a lawsuit—a plaintiff has no authority to challenge the conduct of another individual in court—unless it is *explicitly* asserted *whose*[59] individual rights were violated (who was harmed) because of a

---

59 Some may argue that infraction notices are issued and enforced to protect the general welfare of the people. The problem with this argument is that *if* it cannot be asserted which specific members of the people were being protected with the enforcement of a statute, then it cannot be argued that the statute was being enforced to protect people generally. The whole is made up of its parts.

defendant's conduct.[60] If a defendant has not been alleged to have broken a promise to someone (contract dispute), or caused property or bodily harm to someone (tort), then the defendant cannot be guilty of violating another individual's right to life, liberty, or pursuit of happiness; there can be no standing to file a lawsuit.

[L]ike the prudential component, the constitutional component of standing doctrine incorporates concepts concededly not susceptible of precise definition. The injury alleged must be, for example, **"distinct and palpable,"** Gladstone, Realtors v. Village of Bellwood, 441 US 91 at 100 (1979) (quoting Warth v. Seldin, supra, at 501), and **not "abstract" or "conjectural" or "hypothetical,"** Los Angeles Lyons, 461 US 95 at 101–102 (1983); O'Shea v. Littleton, 414 US 488 at 494 (1974). The injury must be "fairly" traceable to the challenged action, and **relief from injury must be "likely" to follow** from a favorable decision. See Simon v. Eastern Kentucky Welfare Rights Org., US At 38 at 41. <u>Allen v. Wright</u>, 468 U.S. 737 (1984). (emphasis added)

...[C]ourts must look behind names that symbolize the parties to determine whether a justiciable case or controversy is presented <u>United States v. Interstate Commerce Commission</u>, 337 U.S. 426 at 430 (1949).

---

60 Some courts might claim that the state is the injured party. However, assuming there was sufficient evidence to support this notion, the hearing then would have to take place in a federal court instead of a state's court to avoid any conflicts of interest.

Police powers cannot show that anyone was distinctly or palpably harmed as a result of an individual not carrying a photo-ID in their pocket. No one can claim their rights were infringed upon as a result of an individual refusing to wear their seat belt.[61] Lawsuits cannot be grounded on the 'hypothetical-conjecture' that an individual *might* injure someone by traveling too fast (speeding).[62] The state or municipality (city) "when looked beyond its mesmerizing title of authority" has no standing to sue.

Any civil punishment inflicted upon a defendant is supposed to go directly to the party whose individual rights were violated. The purpose is to *relieve*[63] the party who was injured.

---

61 Some may try to argue that seat belt laws are a protection of individual rights: given that all citizens have a right to health care, any citizen that harms themself because they did not wear a seat belt will cost the taxpayers' money. This argument is fallacious for three reasons:

- Civil actions (lawsuits) cannot have standing over a hypothetical injury (e.g., a person *might* cost taxpayers money).
- People do not have an individual or natural right to force one person to labor for care of another; there is no such thing as a natural right to healthcare.
- Mandated health care forces all people to receive occidental (Western) medicine. The individuals' right to life and pursuit of happiness requires that people are free to utilize any form of medicine they want, including Eastern medicine, or if preferred, no medical treatment at all.

62 The exception to the statement above would be if a public nuisance lawsuit was filed by individuals who took the time to assemble testimonies and evidence to show that the defendant routinely demonstrates *negligent* behavior that adversely affects them.

63 *Black's Law Dictionary,* 2d ed., s.v. "relief:...deliverance from oppression, wrong, or injustice."

However, *relief* for an injury is never provided in infraction cases. The money generated from infraction civil actions go directly to the state or municipality (city) to serve as a source of revenue. This goes against the entire intent of civil proceedings; people are being sued over victimless crimes. Infraction cases upon motion (request) ought to be dismissed with prejudice[64] for failure to show a cause of action[65] for which relief can be granted.

---

64 *Black's Law Dictionary*, 2d ed., s.v. "with prejudice: (1) a dismissed case cannot be tried again, (2) court order is final."

65 *Black's Law Dictionary*, 2d ed., s.v. "cause of action:…the right to bring a suit."

ALL INFRACTION COURTS ARE BIASED

One of the maxims of due process of law is that all defendants are entitled to have a disinterested third party or parties serve as triers of fact and law. However, the very nature by which infraction cases are structured prevents defendants from ever acquiring an impartial hearing.

As mentioned previously, money generated from infraction hearings is used as a source of revenue for the state or municipalities (cities).[66] The state or municipalities are the ones that employ the judges who rule on civil infraction proceedings (traffic tickets). Judges necessarily have vested interests in the outcome of their cases; a judge cannot be impartial. If a judge were to rule, impartially, every case as not guilty, that judge would not generate any revenue for his/her agency; that judge would be out of a job! In accordance with federal law, Title 28, U.S.C. § 455, if the impartiality of a judge might be reasonably questioned, the judge is supposed to recuse themself. Yet if all judges did actually recuse themselves, infraction cases would never exist in the first place.

Furthermore, both the complainant (cop) and the judge work for the same agency; they both claim to represent the state or

---

66 Municipalities (cities) are bound to abide by the Constitution and general laws. See addendum 3.

municipality (city) in question. There can be no impartiality from the courts when those judges hearing the court cases are also members of the party filing the complaint.

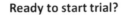

Ready to start trial?

How is this fair? You are all on the same team!

Bias is also evident in the fact that infraction courts require defendants to subpoena (force) a plaintiff to court in order to defend against their accusation(s).

In order for a defendant to be found guilty, the plaintiff in accordance with Washington State infraction court rules (IRLJ rule 3.3 [d]) must demonstrate by a preponderance of the evidence[67] that an offense was committed.

---

67 *Black's Law Dictionary*, 5th ed., s.v. "preponderance of evidence: Evidence which is of greater weight or more convincing than the evidence which is offered in opposition to it; that is, evidence which as a whole shows that the fact sought to be proved is more probable than not. Braud v. Kinchen, La.App., 310 So.2d 657, 659." In other words, preponderance of evidence functionally means greater than 50 percent odds.

RULE IRLJ 3.3
PROCEDURE AT CONTESTED HEARING

(d) Factual Determination. The court shall determine whether the **plaintiff has proved by a preponderance of the evidence** that the defendant committed the infraction. If the court finds the infraction was committed, it shall enter an appropriate order on its records. If the court finds the infraction was not committed, it shall enter an order dismissing the case. (emphasis added)

Since the plaintiff is responsible for showing that an offence likely occurred, it should stand to reason that the plaintiff, also, has the onus of showing up to court and arguing their case—if their case is not to be dismissed. However, contrariwise, infraction courts require defendants to *subpoena* (force) an officer to court if they want to challenge any accusations made against them or avoid being guilty by default. This practice effectively assumes a defendant guilty until proven innocent; agents of government are violating their fiduciary duty[68] by placing the burden of proof upon their beneficiaries.

CITING OFFICER'S TESTIMONY IS "HEARSAY"

Assuming the state had standing to proceed with a civil action, the evidence used to prosecute a person for speeding is inadmissible according to the court's own rules.

---

68   See chapter: "Intent for Government".

In attempts to create a standardized set of procedures for the application of due process, federal courts long ago created a volume of rules known as the *Federal Rules of Evidence*. The Rules of Evidence apply to all federal courts and to every state's courts that chose to adopt the proposed rules.[69]

Federal Rules of Evidence
Rule 101. Scope; Definitions

(a) Scope. These rules apply to proceedings in United States courts. The specific courts and proceedings to which the rules apply, along with exceptions, are set out in Rule 1101.
(b) Definitions. In these rules:

> **(1) "civil case" means a civil action or proceeding;**
>
> (2) "criminal case" includes a criminal proceeding;
>
> (3) "public office" includes a public agency;
>
> (4) "record" includes a memorandum, report, or data compilation;
>
> (5) a "rule prescribed by the Supreme Court" means a rule adopted by the Supreme Court under statutory authority; and
>
> (6) a reference to any kind of written material or any other medium includes electronically stored information.

Washington is one of many states to adopt the Rules of Evidence into practice. Specifically, the Rules of Evidence are said to

---

69 Washington State Courts' Rules of Evidence can be found within the Rules of General Application.

apply to contested hearings for infraction notices as outlined within Washington State court's *Infraction Rules for Courts of Limited Jurisdiction* (IRLJ) rule 3.3 (c).

RULE IRLJ 3.3
PROCEDURE AT CONTESTED HEARING

(c) Rules of Evidence. **The Rules of Evidence and statutes that relate to evidence in infraction cases shall apply to contested hearings.** The court may consider the notice of infraction and any other written report made under oath submitted by the officer who issued the notice or whose written statement was the basis for the issuance of the notice in lieu of the officer's personal appearance at the hearing, unless the defendant has caused the officer to be served with a subpoena to appear in accordance with instructions from the court issued pursuant to rule 2.6(a)(2). (emphasis added)

Within the Rules of Evidence (rule 701), it is said that no witness may testify about an opinion pertaining to technical or otherwise specialized knowledge unless they are an expert witness.[70]

Federal Rules of Evidence
Rule 701. Opinion Testimony by Lay Witnesses

---

70 Washington State's *Rules of Evidence* and the *Federal Rules of Evidence* are essentially synonymous.

If a witness is not testifying as an expert, testimony in the form of an opinion is limited to one that is:
(a) rationally based on the witness's perception;
(b) helpful to clearly understanding the witness's testimony or to determining a fact in issue; and
(c) **not based on scientific, technical, or other specialized knowledge** within the scope of Rule 702. (emphasis added)

Yet within Washington State court rules it is made very obvious that the police officer using the radar gun is not the technical expert. Specifically, IRLJ rule 6.6 (b) references a form that is to serve in lieu of a speed-measuring device (SMD) expert's testimony when the expert is not explicitly subpoenaed to court.

IRLJ 6.6
SPEED MEASURING DEVICE: DESIGN AND CONSTRUCTION CERTIFICATION

(b) Speed Measuring Device Certificate; Form. **In the absence of proof of a request on a separate pleading to produce an electronic or laser speed measuring device (SMD) expert** served on the prosecuting authority and filed with the clerk of the court at least 30 days prior to trial or such lesser time as the court deems proper, a certificate in substantially **the following form is admissible in lieu of an expert witness** in any court proceeding in which the design and construction of an electronic or laser speed measuring device (SMD) is an issue: ... (emphasis added)

A police officer should not testify that he or she has personal knowledge that the defendant was speeding if the police officer relied on a technical device that they are not an expert in; being trained by an expert to calibrate a speed-measuring device (SMD) is not the same as understanding the physics pertinent to the device. This testimony is blatantly against the Rules of Evidence and ought to be inadmissible.

To clarify this point, consider the following: If a citing officer did not use any technical apparatus to measure the velocity of a traveler in question, then the officer could not *definitively* know the velocity of that accused person. If the officer does not definitively know the velocity of an accused person, then the officer cannot have *personal knowledge* of the accused person's speed; he or she would have to *conjecture* (form an *opinion* of) what the accused person's velocity was.

When, however, a citing officer is using a technical apparatus (SMD) to measure velocity, the officer presumably does not know the fundamental principles of the apparatus being used (physics of the SMD). If the officer does not understand the fundamental principles of how the apparatus works, then the officer cannot *personally know* that what the apparatus tells him is true. The officer is merely accepting on faith that the apparatus is accurate because of what that officer has heard other people say about the accuracy of that apparatus—thus, hearsay. Hearsay evidence is inadmissible in court because it denies the defendant the opportunity to cross-examine and critique a witness's observations for accuracy.[71]

Do you know how that radar gun (SMD) gives accurate info?

Nope. My bosses just say to use it.

This is against the rules of evidence! (Rule 701)

---

71 *Black's Law Dictionary,* 2d ed., s.v. "hearsay: A term applied to that species of testimony given by a witness who relates, **not what he knows personally**, but what others have told him, or what he has heard said by others. Ilopt v. Utah, 110 U. S. 574, 4 Sup. Ct. 202. 28 L.Ed. 202; Morellv. Morell, 157 Ind. 170, 00 N. E. 1002; Stockton v. Williams, 1 Doug. (Mich.) 570; People v. Kraft, 01 Hun, 474, 30 N. Y. Supp. 1034. **Hearsay evidence** is that which does not derive its value solely from the credit of the witness, but **rests mainly on the veracity and competency of other persons**. The very nature of the evidence shows its weakness, and it is admitted only in specified cases from necessity. Code Ga. 1882." (emphasis added)

Black's Law Dictionary, 2d ed., s.v. "hearsay evidence: Testimony about out of court statements that are involving someone other than the person that is testifying. It is *inadmissible* because it cannot be cross examined. Civil court will use it as first hand hearsay." (emphasis added)

If a person is not cited for an infraction involving an SMD, they may alternatively ask the citing officer (in court) if they know what the definition of a vehicle is.[72] If an officer does not know that a *vehicle* is defined by *transportation*,[73] then the officer does not know—as a matter of law—what a vehicle is. Consequentially, the officer is incapable of identifying a vehicle and hence cannot assert to have witnessed a driver of a vehicle violating a law. In other words, the citing officer is asserting that people have broken laws that he or she admits to not comprehending.[74] **This demonstrates not only that citing officers lack of probable cause, but also that they commit aggravated perjury.**

TRAFFIC CAMERAS ARE UNCONSTITUTIONAL

The use of unmanned traffic cameras to issue infraction notices is unconstitutional because this practice denies defendants their right to face their accusers.

In accordance with due process of law, any accused person (in a civil or criminal proceeding) is supposed to be allowed to

---

72 As mentioned previously, a few states omit the word *transport* from the definition of vehicle in their codes. Regardless, this technique could just as easily be applied to the terms *violation*, *driver*, or any other term used by the code in question.

73 See chapter "Motor Vehicle Codes (RCW)."

74 Even if an officer happens to know the definition of *transportation*, the officer will still lack evidence to prove the car in question was engaged in transportation.

confront the complainant and cross-examine all evidence used against them (Title 5 U.S.C. § 556 [d]).[75] Included within due process is the opportunity of a defendant to ask questions of any witnesses providing testimony of personal knowledge.

Traffic cameras make it impossible for a defendant to cross-examine the party that is accusing them of wrongdoing—an apparatus can't take the stand and swear to truthfully answer questions. Disregarding due process of law unconstitutionally inhibits a defendant from ensuring their accuser's witness (the apparatus) is not fraudulent or in error.[76]

> Undue restrictions on the right to cross-examine strikes at the very heart of the adversary system: "[a] denial of cross examination without waiver would be a constitutional error of the first magnitude and no amount of showing of want of prejudice would cure it." Brookheart v. Janis, 384 US 1 at 3, 86 S.Ct 1245, 1246, 16 L.Ed.2d 314; Smith v. Illinois, 390 US 129 at 131, 88 S.Ct 748 at 750,

---

75 Some readers may wonder why the confrontation clause for the U.S. Constitution was not cited for this argument. In short, the Constitution's confrontation clause pertains to *criminal proceedings* whereas the code cited above pertains to *all hearings*. Regardless, a reasonable interpretation of due process includes a person's right to face his or her accuser; constitutional provisions are to be liberally interpreted in favor of the beneficiary. See chapter "Intent for Government."

76 Furthermore, in the case of unmanned traffic cameras, there is presumably no actual person filing an infraction notice (complaint) against a defendant; the process is automated. However, if there is never an *actual* individual pleading the courts for *relief,* then the lawsuit cannot be authorized by the Washington State Constitution.

19 L.Ed.2d 956 at 959 (1968); <u>State v. Hanley</u>, 108 Ariz. 144, 148, 493 P.2d 1201 (1972).

...[T]he evidence used to prove the Government's case must be disclosed to the individual so that he has an opportunity to show that it is untrue. While this is important in the case of documentary evidence, it is even more important where the evidence consists of the testimony of individuals whose memory might be faulty or who, in fact, might be perjurers or persons motivated by malice, vindictiveness, intolerance, prejudice, or jealousy. We have formalized these protections in the requirements of confrontation and cross-examination. They have ancient roots. They find expression in the Sixth Amendment which provides that in all criminal cases the accused shall enjoy the right "to be confronted with the witnesses against him." This Court has been zealous to protect these [confrontation] rights from erosion. **It has spoken out not only in criminal cases**, e.g., Mattox v. United States, 156 U.S. 237 at 242–244; Kirby v. United States, 174 U.S. 47; Motes v. United States, 178 U.S. 458 at 474; In re Oliver, 373 U.S. 257 at 273, **but also in all types of cases where administrative and regulatory actions were under scrutiny** [e.g. Southern R. Co. v. Virginia, 290 U.S. 190; Ohio Bell Telephone Co. v. Public Utilities Commission, 301 U.S. 292; Morgan v. United States, 304 U.S. 1 at 19; Carter v. Kubler, 320 U.S. 243; Reilly v. Pinkus, 338 U.S. 269. <u>Greene v. McElroy</u>, 360 U.S. 474, 496-497 (1959)].

An important note: if infraction notices are not contested inside a courtroom but instead responded to via a written statement, the Rules of Evidence do not apply. This is asserted in Washington State court rules IRLJ 3.5 (a).

RULE IRLJ 3.5
DECISION ON WRITTEN STATEMENTS
(Local Option)

(a) Contested Hearings. The court shall examine the citing officer's report and any statement submitted by the defendant. The examination shall take place within 120 days after the defendant filed the response to the notice of infraction. The examination may be held in chambers and **shall not be governed by the Rules of Evidence.**

If the Rules of Evidence do not apply to a contested hearing, then the courts can rule in whatever manner they see fit absent accountability. It is important to contest infraction hearings in court.

MONOPOLIZED PRACTICE AND INTERPRETATION OF LAW

Government prohibits people from practicing law unless they are enrolled into the bar association to ensure that public policies maintain the status quo.

Unless a person has been specifically elected into a bar association from a state's Supreme Court, that person is not permitted to practice law. This can be confirmed, for example, by viewing Washington State court rules, Admission to Practice Rules,[77] rule (1).

APR 1
IN GENERAL; SUPREME COURT; PREREQUISITES
TO THE PRACTICE OF LAW; IMMUNITY

(a) Supreme Court. **The Supreme Court of Washington has the exclusive responsibility and the inherent power to establish the qualifications for admission to practice law, and to admit persons to practice law in this state**. Any person carrying out the functions set forth in these rules is acting under the authority and at the direction of the Supreme Court.

---

77 *Admission to Practice Rules* is a subsection of Washington State Court *Rules of General Application*.

(b) Prerequisites to the Practice of Law. Except as may be otherwise provided in these rules, **a person shall not appear as an attorney or counsel in any of the courts of the State of Washington, or practice law in this state, unless** that person has passed the Washington State bar examination, has complied with the other requirements of these rules, and is an active member of the Washington State Bar Association (referred to in these rules as the Bar Association). A person shall be admitted to the practice of law and become an active member of the Bar Association only by order of the Supreme Court. (emphasis added)

Some may argue that requiring a person to get a permit before they are allowed to work protects the general public from liabilities. As argued in the chapter "Personal Liberty," unalienable rights cannot be deprived from people for any reason short of a trial. *Depriving* a person of their liberty (unalienable right) to work (a feature of pursuing happiness) via licensing and fees is unconstitutional.[78] If a law or rule does not serve to protect or maintain individual rights, then that regulation is not authorized by the constitutions.[79]

---

78 See chapter "Intent for Government."
79 See chapter: "Hypocrisy of Infraction Courts", section: "The State Has No Standing."

Permits established by the Supreme Court create government-granted monopolies to the practice and interpretation of law. In effect, permits do little more than prevent lawyers from challenging established public policy under fear of having their permit—their right to work—revoked.

Do what we say, then you can practice law.

Understood.

8

Confronting Police Power

The first step to defending personal liberty lies in knowing how to interact with police powers[80] when confronted on the public highways.

In theory, there are two general ways a person may defend his or her personal liberty on the highway:

- **Constitutional Defense:** People can notify police of their erroneous conduct when they demand to see a person's papers without a warrant, despite notification that the person is not traveling for hire. This approach, while simple and sincere, generally comes across as

---

80   There is a sharp distinction between *police officers* and *peace officers*. Police officers exist to enforce policy; peace officers exist to enforce peace. Police officers have no duty to serve the public. <u>Warren v. District of Columbia</u>, 444 A.2d 1 (DC Ct. Ap. 1981)

provocative to police and may generate more liability than most people would care to deal with.

- **<u>Amended Documents Defense:</u>** People can freely provide their papers to police upon request, provided they amend their papers in such a way as to avoid implications of being for hire. Instead of asserting the Fourth Amendment to police, individuals wait for their day in court to argue their right to exercise personal liberty or the hypocrisies of the court administration. While less likely to provoke police, this method will require a person to be much more articulate in his or her ability to argue the law in court.

CONSTITUTIONAL DEFENSE

The first method purports that people maintain their constitutional rights from the moment they are confronted by police power and ultimately prosecute police for wrongful conduct.

When a person is first pulled over by a citing officer, they need to assert that they are traveling by right and not by privilege; the officer needs to be informed that the person isn't traveling for hire and therefore cannot be subject to the citing officer's jurisdiction. If the officer persists in demanding a driver's license, the person then acquires the officer's name, badge number, and states that no papers will be provided unless there is a search warrant. As tensions rise, the person either surrenders their papers to the citing officer under threat of arrest (under protest)[81] or allows themself to be arrested and their car to be impounded.[82]

This approach is not recommended for most people. Many police officers know various legal tricks that can be used to harass and falsely incriminate travelers. Anyone not versed in law enforcement antics is at greater risk when confronted by police powers.[83] Additionally, successful challenges to the constitutionality of police conduct can only be done in higher courts. Large amounts of time, money, and cut red tape are required to plead to higher courts.

Anyone who does desire to directly confront police powers ought to possess multiple media recording devices in their personal motorized device to prove that constitutional rights were indeed violated and eliminate any deniability.

---

81 *Black's Law Dictionary,* 5th ed., s.v. "under protest: A payment made or an act done under compulsion while the payer or actor asserts that he waives no rights by making the payment or by doing the act."

82 The Fourth Amendment argument only has standing in court if police powers first threaten an individual with arrest for non-compliance. If the papers are relinquished before arrest is threatened, it can be argued that the papers were consensually provided.

83 This book does not detail the various strategies police use to bully people into submission. Those interested should conduct further independent research in this subject.

AMENDED DOCUMENTS DEFENSE

The second method purports to circumvent police powers and focus energy in the court instead of on the streets. Pursuant to this goal, there are techniques for amending personal documents that avoid any implication of employment; people may freely provide their amended papers to police powers upon request and later in court argue their right to exercise personal liberty.

To begin, people who currently possess a driver's license should enter their local Department of Motor Vehicles and amend their signature so as to explicitly state a reservation of rights. For example, citizens of Washington State can reserve their rights by amending signatures[84] as seen below:

"Without Prejudice" RCW 62A, U.C.C. 1-308
YOUR SIGNATURE

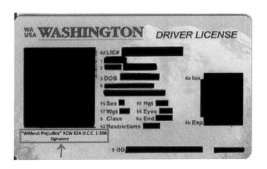

---

84   Your signature must be written below your reservation of rights and the reservation of rights *ought* to have prioritized legibility over your signature.

People out of ignorance (or coercion) submit themselves to the jurisdiction of motor vehicle codes by confessing to the police that they are driving *for hire*—confessions assumed and presumed by police powers through a defendant's forfeiture of a driver's license. By signing a document with the additional terms "without prejudice," or "under protest," and "U.C.C. 1-308",[85] the person signing establishes the retention of any rights he or she unknowingly or under false pretense agrees to surrender. In the illustration above, the amended driver's license implies the signer knows the rules of the road established for employed drivers but does not unknowingly imply the signer to be *for hire*.

Performance or acceptance under reservation of rights.

(a) A party that with explicit reservation of rights performs or promises performance or assents to performance in a manner demanded or offered by the other party does not thereby prejudice the rights reserved. Such words as "without prejudice," "under protest," or the like are sufficient (62A. 1-308).

(b) Subsection (a) of this section does not apply to an accord and satisfaction (2012 c 214 § 122).

---

85   The preface: "RCW 62A." before U.C.C. 1-308 references Washington State's adoption of this code from the Uniform Commercial Code. The Uniform Commercial Code is one of a number of uniform acts promulgated by legal committees to harmonize the law of sales and other commercial transactions in all fifty states within the United States.

Amending a driver's license by itself is not sufficient to prevent self-incrimination. Unamended, a vehicle registration admits its owner to be *using* the device for employment purposes. Specifically, within all vehicle registrations is a box titled "USE" containing a three-or-four letter abbreviation; sedans, for instance, typically label their *use* as "PAS" for passengers.[86] These abbreviations left unchanged imply the registered device to be used primarily for employment purposes.

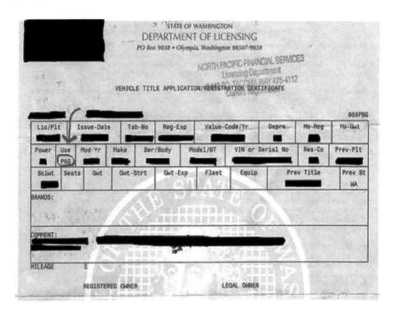

---

86 See appendix 1. The word "passenger" is for-hire terminology.

People should cross out the abbreviation and then amend the "USE" by drawing an arrow away from the box to a newly written term saying "family" or "guest" to prevent this unintended implication. Ideally, people who are not *for hire* would never register their personal motorized devices to become a vehicle. Alas, today's culture provides no other means by which to prove ownership of personal motorized devices.

After personal documents have been amended, it is important to minimize conversation with police powers as much as possible.[87] All conversations by police officers during traffic stops are an attempt to conduct what is legally called *discovery*—efforts to acquire information (or documents) to be used in prosecution of the detained person. Everything a person says in response to discovery questions can and will be construed against them in a court of law.

All responses to questioning should be succinct and tactical if silence is unfeasible.[88] When a police officer does inevitably ask for license and registration, they should be immediately

---

87 Many commonly used words pertaining to motor vehicles carry legal implications of for-hire activity. See appendix 1.

88 Suppose an officer begins a conversation about an infraction by asking, "Going a little fast, weren't you?" If the person replies yes, they acquiesce to the officer's jurisdiction and admit guilt; if the person replies no, the officer can construe the remark as evidence that the person's character is argumentative or fraudulent in nature. The ideal response is to not answer this question, or simply say, "I neither admit nor deny your allegations; I leave you to your strictest proofs."

corrected: "I do not have a driver's license, but I have an amended personal identification demonstrating my proof of competency to travel upon the public highways." The citing officer may not understand what is being said. Regardless, this allows a person to argue in court that they were not admitting to the officer (by handing them ID) to be engaged in for-hire activity.

If a person receives an infraction notice that requires a signature, he or she should not sign it! They should write "Copy Received" instead. It is important to not let a signature on an infraction notice unintentionally admit anything on the signer's behalf.[89] Alternatively, if a police officer threatens to arrest someone for not signing the ticket, that person may write "under protest" in addition to writing his or her signature. Under protest is important because it can lawfully prevent a signature from being used as evidence in court.[90]

This method will likely require people to appeal to higher courts. Lower courts typically dismiss all "renegade" arguments, absent reasoning, on the assumption that most people will not pursue the matter further.

---

89 Signatures written on infraction notices can be used as evidence that the defendant believed the motor vehicle code had jurisdiction over them. It is important never to acquiesce into codes when possible.

90 *Black's Law Dictionary*, 2d ed., s.v. "under protest: The term that means to retain the rights to make an objection later on."

9

Contending Infraction Courts

Being able to articulate the hypocritical administration of motor vehicle laws is important. However, people also need to be aware of the tricks that courts can use to discretely circumvent justice.

COURTS SELECTIVELY NOTICE FACTS

Municipal infraction courtrooms are not required to acknowledge the true intent for a law when making a judgment unless the defendant explicitly mentions the laws.

According to the Rules of Evidence, judges have free discretion to notice any facts they want. Functionally, a court (judge) may turn a blind eye to laws if not explicitly mentioned by the defendant.

RULE ER 201
JUDICIAL NOTICE OF ADJUDICATIVE FACTS

(a) Scope of Rule. This rule governs only judicial notice of adjudicative facts.

(b) Kinds of Facts. A judicially noticed fact must be one not subject to reasonable dispute in that it is either (1) generally known within the territorial jurisdiction of the trial court or (2) capable of accurate and ready determination by resort to sources whose accuracy cannot reasonably be questioned.

(c) When Discretionary. **A court may take judicial notice, whether requested or not.** (emphasis added)

To avoid this situation, a defendant must motion (request from the court) "judicial notice" and cite the laws needed for legal defense.

RULE ER 201
JUDICIAL NOTICE OF ADJUDICATIVE FACTS

(d) When Mandatory. **A court shall take judicial notice if requested by a party and supplied with the necessary information.**

(e) Opportunity To Be Heard. A party is entitled upon timely request to an opportunity to be heard as to the propriety of taking judicial notice and the tenor of the matter noticed. In the absence of prior notification, the request may be made after judicial notice has been taken.

(f) Time of Taking Notice. **Judicial notice may be taken at any stage of the proceeding.** (emphasis added)

When a person requests judicial notice, the judge must consider the law being presented as long as legal citations are made available in a timely manner. Any time people wish to make a judge take notice of laws ranging from the Constitution to court rules, it is important to demand judicial notice on the record. Judicial notice can take place at any time during a hearing.

JUSTIFICATION OF JUDGE RULINGS

Despite courts' excuses for concealing the grounds of a judge's ruling, courts, by law, are required to be transparent in any and all decisions they make.

Many judges, when confronted the with legal arguments presented in this book, will attempt to ignore the person and not justify their rulings as they continue hearing (refuse to dismiss) the case. Some judges will claim they cannot explain their ruling as they are not allowed to give "legal advice." Other judges will go so far as to say they do not have to provide their grounds for ruling.

Lawfully, judges are not supposed to omit the grounds for the rulings they make. It is against the Washington State Constitution and common law; justice is supposed to be administered *openly*.

Wash. Const. art. I, § 10
SECTION 10 ADMINISTRATION OF JUSTICE. Justice in all cases shall be administered openly, and without unnecessary delay.

Openly does not simply mean anyone can walk into the courtroom during a hearing. It means that judges are to be transparent in their rulings so that the public may observe how they are in accordance with their constitution. If the public cannot be made aware as to why a judge ruled the way they did, then there is no point in allowing the public to observe courtrooms in the first place.[91] This constitutional rule was made as a safeguard to protect people from tyranny. Furthermore, rationale for judgments is supposed to be

---

91   In 2010, some legislators proposed a bill named the Idaho Right to Constitutional Government Act, which mandated that any state law created by legislators in the future had to directly show how it was in alignment with constitutional provisions. This bill never passed. It is important to know how a statute is derived from a constitution to prevent representatives from abusing power.

provided during a case for appellate courts to critique later should a case ever be appealed.

> "While district court's decision to seal court documents is reviewed only for abuse of discretion, it is imperative that district court articulate its reasons for electing to seal or not to seal a record; without full explanation, Court of Appeals is unable to review the district court's exercise of discretion." E.E.O.C. v. National Children's Center, 98 F.3d 1406 at 1407 (D.C. Cir 1996)

Never assume that court orders are sanctioned by law; people should always demand citations for jurisdiction.

> ...[J]urisdiction may [not] be maintained by mere averment, or that the party asserting jurisdiction may be relieved of his burden

by any formal procedure. If his allegations of jurisdictional facts are challenged by his adversary in any appropriate manner, he must support them by competent proof. And, where they are not so challenged, the court may still insist that the jurisdictional facts be established, or the case be dismissed, and, for that purpose, the court may demand that the party alleging jurisdiction justify his allegations by a preponderance of evidence. <u>McNutt v General Motors Acceptance</u>, 56 S.Ct. 502, 298 U.S.189 (1936).

For instance, it shouldn't be assumed that it is lawful for judges to order people to turn off their video recording devices in court (under threat of contempt). People should ask judges what state law or court rules gives them authority to make such an order. Unless that judge can show how their order is (1) not a violation of an individual's right to open justice and (2) protecting someone's individual rights, the judge's order is unlawful and leaves them liable.[92]

FILING DOCUMENTS
People need to be extremely careful in handling all of their legal documents to avoid unintended legal consequences.

---

92 Judges can be prosecuted if it can be proven that they have violated a provision in the declaration of rights. In this case, it would be argued that the right to open justice, Article 1, § 10, was being violated in prohibiting camcorder use. See addendum 3.

People should never sign any infraction notices or other court papers unless they understand the full ramifications of signing. They should write "Copy Received" instead. **Signing a plea of not guilty can legally imply that the signer believes the law has jurisdiction over them.**[93] Instead of mailing a signed copy of an infraction notice to courts, people should go to the court of jurisdiction in person and request a hearing date in demurrer. [94]

Additionally, it is important to **record everything**! It does not matter how glorious a person's legal defense is if that person has no record of documents or attendance. The courts can lie and say the defendant failed to meet his or her obligations.

If a person speaks with court staff, they should be sure to get the name of the staffer and document the time of the conversation. If a person undergoes a court hearing, that person should make sure to *immediately* acquire an official copy of the court hearing; preferably the day of the hearing. If a person waits

---

93 "It is essential to a valid trial that in some way there should be an issue between the [state] and the [accused], and without a plea, there could be no issue." United States v. Aurandt, 107 Pac. 1064, 1065 (N.M. 1910).

94 *Black's Law,* 2d ed., s.v. "demurrer: … an allegation that, even if the facts as stated in the pleading to which objection is taken to be true, yet their legal consciences are not such as to put the demurring party to the necessity of answering them or proceeding further with the cause."

to acquire a record, the hearings can be erased leaving people without proof of what happened in court.

FOUL PLAY

It is important to acknowledge that courts will not play fair. While a presiding judge does not necessarily have vested interests in a particular traffic ticket being won or lost, judges do have vested interests in ensuring that traffic tickets are issued *generally*. When the integrity of disseminating traffic tickets is confronted, judges will have no issues making up rules or blatantly ignoring arguments in order to browbeat defendants into submission.

Judges don't respond favorably to the contentions raised in this book. Arguments raised in court may be subject to strawmanning or dismissed without rebuttal and ruled as "nonsensical." Attempts to submit evidence may be explicitly denied despite a motion for judicial notice. Courtrooms may summon police to intimidate individuals if they do not "fall in line."

The fact of this matter is this: even if people dot all their i's and cross all their t's, the courts do not play fair. Courts can only be held accountable if more people fight their traffic tickets and more people prudently observe and object to the system. Public outcry is the only action that will cause the courts to act with a conscience.

Conclusion

There is an old wives' tale that says if a frog is placed directly into hot water, that frog will immediately and relentlessly attempt to escape. However, if the frog is placed into cool water that is slowly heated to boiling temperatures, the frog will consensually remain in the pan until it boils to death. I've come to believe that through gradual conditioning, people have come to accept infringements on liberty that in generations past would have never been tolerated.

People should feel encouraged to fight their traffic tickets in court. Even if an individual feels certain that his or her court case will be lost, they should still take the time to object to the unlawful practices on the record. Courtrooms should be forced to expend their resources (time and personnel) in taking money; people should not blindly write checks simply because a cop accused them of wrongdoing.

Courts rely on the fact that very few people contest infraction notices issued to them. If more people took the time to contest their infraction notices in court, the ticketing system would become unsustainable, as authorities simply could not allot the resources necessary to offer everyone a day in court.

People should not be forced to obtain a license (ask permission) to exercise their right to travel. Nor should people be forced to purchase any services or forfeit constitutional rights as a condition to exercise the right to travel. I am fearful that if these current public policies continue unchecked, our liberty to exercise our rights (to travel or otherwise) will irrevocably, through permitting/licensing, become subject to the will of a tyrannical government.

If we do not safeguard our ability to *effectively* come and go as we see fit, without needing a gatekeeper's permission, we will inexorably have our freedom—our lives—destroyed. If our ability to travel upon public highways is taken away, our ability to effectively defend any other natural or civil right shall be taken with it.

Addendum 1: Misinterpretation of Law

When researching any legal term, it is important to not accept at face value the first definition provided.[95] Many legal terms over the years have been paraphrased in ways that mislead the public as to the word's true meanings.

To highlight the fact that legal definitions have been convoluted, the term *driver* shall be examined:

Blacks Law Dictionary 6th edition
Driver
A person actually **doing driving**, whether employed by owner to drive vehicle or driving his own vehicle.

---

95   To see how terms are legally defined, see chapter: "Reading and Arguing Law."

On first glance, people may assume that the definition of a driver refers to a person who drives on his or her own accord (personal vehicle) or as a means of employment (employed by owner). However, those who examine the sentence more closely will find that the definition above is conspicuous. Why would the dictionary say *doing driving* instead of simply saying a person driving? What is the significance of the word *doing*?

> **Black's Law Dictionary, 2nd ed.**
> **Doing**
> The formal word by which services were reserved and expressed in old conveyances; as "rendering" (reddendo) was expressive of rent.

The term *doing* was an expression used in earlier times, which meant to express that a service was being provided. A driver is not merely someone who is driving, but someone who is driving as a service. To clarify this issue, people may cite older editions of Black's Law Dictionary to reference the term *driver*:

> **Black's Law Dictionary, 4th ed.**
> **Driver**
> One employed in conducting or operating a coach, carriage, wagon, or other vehicle, with horses, mules, or other animals, or a bicycle,

tricycle, or motor car, though not a street railroad car. **A person actually doing driving whether employed by owner to drive or driving his own vehicle**. (emphasis added)

Black's Law Dictionary, 3rd ed.
Driver

One employed in conducting or operating a coach, carriage, wagon, or other vehicle, with horses, mules, or other animals, or a bicycle, tricycle, or motor car, though not a street railroad car. See David v. Petrinovich 112 Ala. 654. 21 So. 344, 36 L.R.A. 615; Isaacs v. Railroad Co., 7 Am. Rep. 418, 47 N.Y. 122.

Upon citing older editions of the dictionary, it is discovered that a *driver* explicitly means one who is employed or travels as a business. The sentence phrasing *doing driving* was constructed to qualify that drivers were employed to provide a service.[96] The definition of driver in Black's Law Dictionary, 6th edition, was abstracted from the principal definition and not cited with its respective case law, distorting the term's true meaning.

There are many publications besides dictionaries for citing case law when researching a legal term in question. For example, there is a volume called the *Federal Digest* that contains a series of books titled *Words and Phrases*. In these books are citations to federal case law categorized by subject matter. Similarly,

---

96 "Driver" could be either an employee or employer using a vehicle for contractual purposes.

states have their own state digests that cite that state's case law. Alternatively, there are legal encyclopedias including *American Jurisprudence* (Am Jur) and *Corpus Juris Secundum* (CJS). Multiple accredited legal resources (newer and older) should be studied to avoid misconceptions.

Addendum 2: Motor Vehicle Codes Continued

Some readers may prove skeptical about the interpretation of the term *vehicle* asserted in the body of the book. If motor vehicle is defined as a *for hire* device, then why would motor vehicle codes separately define *for hire vehicles,* and why do commercial driver's licenses exist?

Compensation Drivers

Motor vehicle codes provide separate definitions for the terms *vehicle* and *for hire vehicle*:

> **RCW 46.04.190**
> **For hire vehicle.**
> "For hire vehicle" means any motor vehicle used for the transportation of persons for *compensation*, except auto stages and ride-sharing vehicles. (emphasis added)

At first glance, people may assume the codes distinguish between those who use the highways for hire and those that don't. This is a misconception revealed by the definition of *compensation*:

> **Black's Law Dictionary, 2d ed.**
> **Compensation**
> Indemnification; payment of damages; making amends;...The word also signifies the remuneration or wages given to an employee or officer. But it is not exactly synonymous with "salary." See Teople v. Wemple, 115 N. Y. 302, 22 N. E. 272; Com. v. Carter, 55 S. V. 701, 21 Ivy. Law Rep. 1509; Crawford County v. Lindsay, 11 111. App. 201; Ivilgore v. People, 70 111. 548.

Compensation is a specific term that implies being reimbursed for any damages incurred as a result of being for hire. In other words, there is a difference between a device that is used to fulfill contractual obligations and a device that also receives payment to compensate for "wear and tear" and mileage. Commercial trucks, for instance, would classify as *for hire vehicles* because they are reimbursed for each mile they travel. In contrast, pizza delivery cars may only classify as a *vehicle* if the driver is required to pay the cost of transportation themselves.

COMMERCIAL DRIVER'S LICENSE

If *vehicle* legally means a motorized device that may be used for hire, then what are commercial driver's licenses for?

Commerce is a legal term specifically meaning trade or transportation among nations or states—participation in *interstate* affairs. In other words, commerce is a term that implies that people are crossing state or federal borders to conduct contractual obligations.

Black's Law Dictionary, 2d ed.
Commerce

The words "commerce" and "trade" are synonymous, but not identical. They are often used interchangeably; but, strictly speaking, commerce relates to intercourse or dealings with foreign nations, states, or political communities, while trade denotes business intercourse or mutual traffic within the limits of a state or nation, or the buying, selling, and exchanging of articles between members of the same community. See Hooker v. Vandewater, 4 Denio (N. Y.) 353, 47 Am. Dec. 258; Jacob; Wharton

According to the U.S. Constitution, Congress has the right to regulate interstate commerce as it sees fit. Any person who wants to conduct *large-scale* trade or transportation between state or country borders must acquire special *commercial* licensing from the federal government.

U.S. Const., Art 1, § 8., cl 3

[The Congress shall have power] To regulate commerce with foreign nations, and among the several states, and with the Indian tribes. (emphasis added)

In contrast, unclassified driver's licenses are permits granted by the government to use public highways for smaller-scale transportation not explicitly crossing borders of a state—*intrastate* employment.

ADDENDUM 3: OATH OF OFFICE

Many government agency positions (federal or state) require an inauguration that mandates swearing an oath to the constitution(s).

As mentioned within the chapter, "Law in the United States," the U.S. Constitution is *the supreme law of the land,* as stated in article VI, paragraph 2.

> ...[A] law repugnant to the constitution is void; and that *courts,* as well as other departments, are bound by that instrument. Marbury v. Madison, 5 U.S. 137 (1803).

> An unconstitutional act is not a law; it confers no rights; it imposes no duties; it affords no protection; it creates no office; it is, in legal contemplation, as inoperative as though it had never been passed. Norton v. Shelby County, 118 U.S. 425 (1886).

Government officials who are elected into authority must swear an oath to support the Constitution as mandated by the Constitution:[97]

U.S. Const. art. VI, cl. 3.

Oath of Office: The Senators and Representatives before mentioned, and the Members of the several State Legislatures, and all executive and judicial Officers, both of the United States and of the several States, shall be bound by Oath or Affirmation, to support this Constitution.

For example, RCW 43.01.020 references the oath or affirmation required for the governor of Washington State to take office:

RCW 43.01.020

Oath of office.

The governor, lieutenant governor, secretary of state, treasurer, auditor, attorney general, superintendent of public instruction, commissioner of public lands, and insurance commissioner, shall, before entering upon the duties of their respective offices, take and subscribe an oath or affirmation in substance as follows: I do solemnly swear (or affirm) that I will support the Constitution of the United States and the Constitution and laws of the state of Washington, and that I will faithfully discharge the duties of the office of (name of office) to the best of my ability.

---

97   See also: U.S. Const., *art II, §1, cl. 8.*

The oath or affirmation shall be administered by one of the justices of the supreme court at the capitol. A certificate shall be affixed thereto by the person administering the oath, and the oath or affirmation so certified shall be filed in the office of the secretary of state before the officer shall be qualified to discharge any official duties: PROVIDED, that the oath of the secretary of state shall be filed in the office of the state auditor.

Here are a few other codes for Washington State mandating an oath of office:

Attorney general, oath of office: RCW 43.10.010.
Court commissioners, oath of office: RCW 2.24.020.
Horse racing commission, oath of office: RCW 67.16.012.
Judges of superior court, oath of office: Wash. Const., art. IV, § 28; RCW 2.08.080, 2.08.180.
Judges of supreme court, oath of office: Wash. Const., art. IV, § 28; RCW 2.04.080.
Liquor control board, oath of office: RCW 66.08.014.
Militia, oath of office: RCW 38.12.150, 38.12.160.
Oaths, mode of administering: Wash. Const., art. 1, § 6.
Perjury, oath defined: RCW 9A.72.010.
State administrative officers, oath required: RCW 43.17.030.
State auditor, oath of office: RCW 43.09.010.
State treasurer, oath of office: RCW 43.08.020.

All police officers are obligated to abide by the constitutions.[98]

Black's Law Dictionary, 5th ed.
Police Power
The power of the State to place restraints on the personal free-dom and property rights of persons for the protection of the public safety, health, and morals or the promotion of the public convenience and general prosperity. The police power is subject to limitations of the federal and state constitutions, and especially to the requirement of due process. Police power is the exercise of the sovereign right of a government to promote order, safety, health, morals and general welfare within constitutional limits and is an essential attribute of government. Marshall v. Kansas City, Mo., 355 S.W.2d 877 at 883. (emphasis added)

Cities, also, are bound by the state constitution. Many large cities have a municipal code with a document that is re-ferred to as a "city charter." Within this legal document (the charter),[99] a city promises to be in accordance with the federal and state constitutions in addition to the general laws of its respective state. For example, the Tacoma City Charter must be in accordance with article XI, § 10 of the Washington State Constitution:

---

98 See appendix 5.

99 Smaller cities are referred to as noncharter code cities within their municipal codes. The terms are nearly synonymous except that charter cities have more le-niencies to create their own legislation than noncharter cities.

Wash. Const. art. XI, § 10
Corporations for municipal purposes shall not be created by special laws;... [they] shall be permitted to frame a charter for its own government, consistent with and subject to the Constitution and laws of this state...

Tacoma City Charter
Article 1 section 1.2
The city shall have all powers now or hereafter granted to like cities *by* **the constitution and laws of the state**, and all powers implied thereby, and shall have and exercise all municipal rights, powers, function, privileges and immunities except as prohibited by law or by this charter. The City may acquire property within or without its corporate limits for any city purpose by purchase, condemnation, lease, gift, and devise and may hold or dispose of such property as the interests of the city may require. No enumeration of particular powers by this charter shall be deemed to be exclusive. (emphasis added)

Within a city's charter are listed various powers: the right to have a police department, the right to have a fire department, the right to have a city hall, and so on. If that city is not in accordance with the federal and state constitutions in addition to the general laws of its state, then the charter does not have any rights and powers. In other words, that charter is in violation of its contract; it is in violation of the franchise. The city waives its right to be a city![100]

---

100 If a charter can be explicitly proven to have violated a person's constitutional rights, there are special forms within legal encyclopedias people can use to revoke the charter's franchise. Those interested should research *writ of mandamus* and *quo warranto.*

Any individual—sworn government official[101] or not—who deprives people of their rights through color of law (pretense of law) is subject to being sued, fined, and imprisoned in accordance with Title 18 U.S.C. sections 241, 242 and Title 42 U.S.C. § 1983, 1985, & 1986.[102] No emergency can justify the violation of any of the provisions of the U.S. Constitution.[103]

> ...[M]unicipalities have no immunity from damages liability flowing from their constitutional violations. <u>Owen v. Independence</u>, 100 S.C.T. 1398 (1980).

> *Edelman v. Jordan*, 415 U.S. 651 at 675, 94 S.Ct. 1347 at 1362, 39 L.Ed.2d 662 (1974). *5 *Monell v. New York City Dept. of Social Services*, 436 U.S. 658 at 700–701, 98 S.Ct. 2018 at 2040–2041, 56 L.Ed.2d 611 (1978),...**reasoned that "there can be no doubt that § 1 of the Civil Rights Act [of 1871] was intended to provide a remedy, to be broadly construed, against all forms of official violation of federally protected right**s." <u>Maine v. Thiboutot,</u> 448 U.S. 1 (1980). (emphasis added)

> Emergency does not create power. Emergency does not increase granted power or remove or diminish the restrictions imposed upon power granted or reserved. The Constitution was adopted in a period of grave emergency. Its grants of power to the federal government and its limitations of the power of the States were

---

101   For punishment toward government agents who are treasonous to the Constitution, see: 18 U.S.C. § 2381.

102   See also 16 Am Jur 2d § 104 (2011).

103   See also 16 Am Jur 2d § 52 (2011).

determined in the light of emergency, and they are not altered by emergency. <u>U.S. v. Cruikshank</u>, 92 U.S. 542 (1938).

Oftentimes, lower courts will attempt to claim that they acted in good faith so they cannot be sued; this is not true. A person's right to bring a lawsuit (right of action) is created simply based on violations of law or constitutional provisions. If a person successfully demonstrates that their constitutional rights were violated through color of law (pretense of law), that person is entitled to reimbursement for any harm done. Judges are deemed to know the constitution and swear to uphold it in their oath or affirmation.

ADDENDUM 4: "HIRED GUNS" ARE UNCONSTITUTIONAL.

An unspoken truth about the *armed* city police in Washington State is that their very existence is not authorized by the Washington State Constitution's Declaration of Rights. [104]

Generally, cities within Washington State have an armed police force; it is not an uncommon sight to see a handgun holstered at the hip of police officers hired by the city. However, it is important to know that cities are defined as being a (municipal) corporation.

> **Black's Law Dictionary, 2d ed.**
> **City**
> A city Is a municipal corporation of a larger class, the distinctive feature of whose organization is its government by a chief executive (usually called "mayor") and a legislative body, composed of representatives of the citizens, (usually called a "council" or "board

---

104 The 'Declaration of Rights' in a state constitution functions similarly to the 'Bill of Rights' in the U.S. Constitution.

of aldermen,") and other officers having special functions. Wight
Co. v. Wolff, 112 Ga. 169, 37 S. E. 395.

The Washington State Constitution does not authorize any
corporation to employ an armed body of men.[105]

Wash. Const. art. I, § 24
RIGHT TO BEAR ARMS. The right of the individual citizen to bear
arms in defense of himself, or the state, shall not be impaired, but
**nothing in this section shall be construed as authorizing in-
dividuals or corporations to organize, maintain or employ an
armed body of men.** (emphasis added)

The Washington State Constitution does not authorize corporations to employ "armed bodies of men." Cities, by definition,
are a corporation. Therefore, cities do not have authority to hire
an armed body of men (armed police force); doing so necessarily violates the authority delegated to cities by the Washington
State Constitution.

Armed city police are outside the authority granted to them
by law. Police powers cannot have authority to enforce laws

---

105 That last clause in art. I, § 24 was intended to counteract the notorious
business practice (at that era) of hiring armed "Pinkertons" to break up labor
unions. In principle, the clause was created to prevent corporations from oppress-
ing the people. Reference: *Robert F. Utter, Hugh D. Spitzer*: The Washington State
Constitution 2nd ed. (page 8).

until they are first within the boundaries of the law themselves. Police powers must respect their fiduciary duty.[106]

---

106   See chapter "Intent for Government."

ADDENDUM 5: *STARE DECISIS* IS RULE BY OLIGARCHY.

Stare Decisis is the principle that every judge is obligated to rule each case in such a way that they are in accordance with the opinions of the highest courts and how they have ruled on similar cases in the past.

Proponents argue that Stare Decisis ensures all courts of law treat people as consistently as possible. The principle of Stare Decisis is firmly adhered to by virtually everyone who is a legal practitioner. However, there is no constitutional provision or other lawful authority mandating individuals to adhere to Stare Decisis.

Originally, lower courts were never *required*, or mandated, to adhere to precedent (case law). At most, precedent was referenced in attempts to be persuasive, but judges were free to disagree. When higher courts made rulings, their rulings would be authoritative over *that* case only; it would not dictate how other courts must rule on their cases in the future. These facts were held as true and commonplace during the founding fathers' generation.

> ...we would have to conclude that the generation of the Framers had a much stronger view of precedent than we do. In fact, as we explain below, **our concept of precedent today is far stricter than that which prevailed at the time of the Framing**. The Constitution does not contain an express prohibition against issuing nonprecedential opinions because the Framers would have seen nothing wrong with the practice. <u>Hart v. Massanari</u>, 266 F.3d 1155 (9th Cir. 2001).

The idea that everyone must abide by the opinions of the highest-ranking judges effectively turns those judges into miniature kings; in effect, the highest-ranking judges dictate how and which laws will be upheld—usurping the legislative branch. This stands contrary to the principles written in the Declaration of Independence and is a violation of the Constitution's division of powers.[107]

---

107 Judiciaries (bench trials) are not always to be the ultimate determiner of a person's guilt or how controversies are resolved. The seventh amendment of the U.S. Constitution grants people the right to a trial by jury in civil cases; a panel of impartial men derived from the local populace by the conflicting parties to decide an appointed case.

Judges are not authorized to freely interpret laws anyway they see fit; they are delegated to judge the best resolution to a dispute in accordance with the intended purpose for our government and statutes. If there is any doubt as to how the judiciary should rule, or if a statute violates the declared intent for government, their rulings should liberally favor the individual's unalienable rights.

> Constitutional provisions for the security of person and property are to be liberally construed, and "it is the duty of courts to be watchful for the constitutional rights of the citizen, and against any stealthy encroachments thereon." <u>Byars v. U.S.</u>, 273 U.S. 28 (1927).

Appendix 1: Definitions

TABLE OF MOTOR VEHICLE DEFINITIONS

RCW 46.04.320

"**Motor vehicle**" means every **vehicle** that is self-propelled and every vehicle that is propelled by electric power obtained from overhead trolley wires, but not operated upon rails.

RCW 46.04.670

"**Vehicle**" includes every device capable of being moved upon a public highway and in, upon, or by which any persons or property is or may be **transported** or drawn upon a public highway, including bicycles.

Blacks Law Dictionary 5th edition

Transportation: The movement of goods or persons from one place to another, by a **carrier.**

Blacks Law Dictionary 5th edition

Carrier: Individual or organization engaged in transporting passengers or goods **for hire.**

"Carrier" means any person engaged in the transportation of passengers or property by land, as a common, contract, or private carrier, or freight forwarder as those terms are used in the Interstate Commerce Act, and officers, agents, and employees of such carriers 18 U.S.C.A. § 831.

OTHER EMPLOYMENT DEFINITIONS:

49 U.S. Code § 32901 – Definitions

Automobile: ...[M]eans a 4-wheeled **vehicle** that is propelled by fuel, or by alternative fuel, manufactured primarily for use on public streets, roads, and highways...

Black's Law Dictionary, 3d ed.

Driver: One employed in conducting or operating a coach, carriage, wagon, or other **vehicle**, with horses, mules, or other animals, or a bicycle, tricycle, or motor car, though not a street railroad car. See Davis v. Petrinovich, 112 Ala 654, 21 So 344, 36 L.R.A. 615; Isaacs v. Railroad Co., 7 Am. Rep 418, 47 N.Y. 122.

Black's Law Dictionary, 2d ed.

Passenger: A person whom a common **carrier** has **contracted** to carry from one place to another, and has, in the course of the performance of that contract, received under his care either upon the means of conveyance, or at the point of departure of that means of conveyance. Bricker v. Philadelphia & R. R. Co., 132 Pa. 1, 18 Atl. 983, 19 Am. St. Rep. 585; Schepers v. Union De-pot R. Co., 126 Mo. 665, 29 S. W. 712; Pennsylvania R. Co. v. Price, 96 Pa. 256; The Main v. Williams, 152 U. S. 122, 14 Sup. Ct. 486, 38 L. Ed. 381 ; Norfolk & W. R. Co. v. Tanner, 100 Va. 379, 41 S. E. 721.

Black's Law Dictionary, 5th ed.

Traffic: Commerce; trade; sale or exchange of merchandise, bills, money, and the like. The passing of goods or commodities from one person to another for an equivalent in goods or money. The subjects of transportation on a route, as persons or goods; the passing to and fro of persons, animals, vehicles, or vessels, along a route of transportation, as along a street, highway, etc. See **commerce.** Senior v. Ratterman, 44 Ohio St. 673, 11 N.E. 321; People v. Horan, 293 Ill. 314, 127 N.E. 673 at 674; People v Dunford, 207 N.Y. 17, 100 N.E. 433, 434; Fine v. Morgan, 74 Fla. 417, 77 So. 533 at 538; Bruno v. U.S. (C.C.A) 289 F. 649 at 655.

Operator: It will be observed from the language of the ordinance that a distinction is to be drawn between the terms 'operator' and 'driver'; the 'operator' of the service car being the person who is licensed to have the car on the streets in the **business of carrying passengers for hire;** while the 'driver' is the one who actually drives the car. However, in the actual prosecution of business, it was possible for the same person to be both 'operator' and 'driver.' Newbill v. Union Indemnity Co., 60 SE.2d 658.

Washington State Digest, 2d "words and phrases"
Use: Wash. 1941. The word "use" or "used" means **to employ or be employed** or occupied, in which sense it includes a single isolated instance of use, and also to practice customarily or, in the case of a place or thing, to be the subject of customary practice, employment or occupation. - Smith v. Northern Pac. Ry. Co., 110 P.2d 851, 7 Wash.2d 652.

Washington State Digest 2d "words and phrases"
Or: Wash. 1939. An indictment or **information may employ conjunctive "and" where the statute uses "or," and will not therefore be subject to demurrer** as insufficient to inform accused of what he is charged with. Rem.Rev.Stat. § 2055. - State v. Rooney, 97 P.2d 156, 2 Wash.2d 17. -Ind & Inf 125(20).

Appendix 2: Supplementary Court Cases

Public Roads are Public Right:

Even the Legislature has no power to deny to a citizen the right to travel upon the highway and transport his property in the ordinary course of his business or pleasure, though this right may be regulated in accordance with the public interest and convenience. Where one undertakes, however, to make a greater use of the public highways for his own private gain, as by the operation of a stagecoach, an omnibus, a truck, or a motorbus, the state may not only regulate the use of the vehicles on the highway, but may prohibit it. Chicago Motor Coach v. Chicago, 169 N.E. 22 (1929).

The right of the Citizen to travel upon the public highways and to transport his property thereon, in the ordinary course of life and business, is a common right which he has under the right to enjoy life and liberty, to acquire and possess property, and to pursue happiness and safety. It includes the right, in so doing, to use the ordinary and usual conveyances of the day, and under the existing modes of travel, includes the right to drive a horse drawn carriage or wagon thereon or to operate an automobile thereon, for the usual and ordinary purpose of life and business. Thompson v. Smith, supra; Teche Lines v. Danforth, Miss., 12 S.2d 784 (1943).`

Our court has stressed the basic right of the transient public and abutting property owners to the free passage of vehicles on public highways and the paramount function of travel as overriding all other subordinate uses of our streets State v. Perry, 130 N.W.2d 343 (1964).

The term "public highway," in its broad popular sense, includes toll roads—any road which the public have a right to use even conditionally, though in a strict legal sense it is restricted to roads which are wholly public. Weirich v. State, 140 Wis. 98. (1909).

As we understand it, the statute does not require a suspect to give the officer a driver's license or any other document. Provided that the suspect either states his name or communicates it to the officer by other means–a choice, we assume, that the suspect may make—the statute is satisfied and no violation occurs. Hiibel v. Sixth Judicial Dist. Court of Nev., 124 S.Ct. 2451 at 2457 (2004).

Before a road is a public road, it must be used by the public generally as a matter of right. Atchison, T. & S. F. Ry. Co. v. Acosta, 435 S.W.2d 539 (1968).

For-Hire versus Non-For-Hire Travel:
The right of a citizen to travel upon the highway and transport his property thereon, in the ordinary course of life and business,

differs radically and obviously from that of one who makes the highway his place of business and uses it for private gain, in the running of a stage coach or omnibus. The former is the usual and ordinary right of a citizen, a common right, a right common to all, while the latter is special, unusual, and extraordinary. As to the former, the extent of legislative power is that of regulation; but, as to the latter, its power is broader. The right may be wholly denied, or it may be permitted to some and denied to others, because of its extraordinary nature. This distinction, elementary and fundamental in character, is recognized by all the authorities: <u>Ex Parte Dickey</u>, (Dickey v. Davis), 85 S.E. 781 (1915).

In State v. Johnson, 75 Mont. 240, 243 P. 1073, we considered the constitutionality of the statute, and after considering the question as to whether it constituted a violation of section 1 of article 4 of the Constitution, as being an unwarranted delegation of legislative power, Mr. Justice Matthews, speaking for the court, said: 'Nor does it violate section 3 or section 14 of article 3 of the state Constitution, nor the Fourteenth Amendment to the Constitution of the United States, securing to the people the right of acquiring, possessing, and enjoying property, and prohibiting the taking of private property for public use or without due process of law, for, while a citizen has the right to travel upon the public highways and to transport his property thereon, that right does not extend to the use of the highways, either in whole or in part, as a place of business for private gain. For the latter purpose no person has a vested right in the use of the highways of the state, but is a privilege or license which the Legislature may grant or withhold in its discretion, or which it may grant upon such conditions as it may see fit to impose, provided the imposition applies impartially. <u>Willis v. Buck</u>, 81 Mont. 472, 263 P. 982 (1928).

Public highways and streets are constructed and maintained at the public expense. No person, therefore, can insist that he has, or may acquire, a vested right to use such streets and highways in carrying on a commercial business. Ex Parte Sterling, 53 S.W.2d 294 (1932).

Washington State Court Cases:
... [F]or while a Citizen has the Right to travel upon the public highways and to transport his property thereon, that Right does not extend to the use of the highways, either in whole or in part, as a place for private gain. For the latter purpose, no person has a vested right to use the highways of the state, but is a privilege or a license which the legislature may grant or withhold at its discretion. State v. Johnson, 243 P. 1073 (1926).

The right of a citizen to travel upon the highway and transport his property thereon in the ordinary course of life and business differs radically and obviously from that of one who makes the highway his place of business and uses it for private gain... State v. City of Spokane, 186 P. 864 (1920).

For hire' vehicles, as provided in section 6313, Rem. Comp. Stats., are defined to mean all motor vehicles other than automobile stages used for the transportation of persons for which transportation remuneration of any kind is received, either directly or indirectly. International Motor Transit Co. v. Seattle, 251 P. 120 (1926).

Complete freedom of the highways is so old and well established a blessing that we have forgotten the days of the 'Robber Barons' and toll roads and yet, under an act like this, arbitrarily administered, the highways may be completely monopolized. If, through lack of interest, the people submit, then they may look to see the most sacred of their liberties taken from them one by one by more or less rapid encroachment. <u>Robertson v. Department of Public Works</u>, 180 Wash 133, 147 (1937).

In State v. White, 97 Wash.2d 92, 640 P.2d 1061 (1982), the supreme court declared that sections 1 and 2 of RCW 9A.76.020 were unconstitutional. While the police may briefly detain a suspect based upon a reasonable suspicion and ask various questions, including the suspect's identity, "a detainee's refusal to disclose his name, address, and other information cannot be the basis of an arrest" State v. White, supra at 106, 640 P.2d 1061. Accordingly, the arrest of the defendant for refusing to give the Snohomish County sheriff his name was unlawful. See State v. Swaite, 33 Wash. App. 477, 656 P.2d 520 (1982). <u>State v. Hoffman</u>, 664 P.2d 1259, 35 Wash. App. 13 at 16, 664 P.2d 1259 (1983).

Police Powers and Jurisdiction:

...[A] detainee's refusal to disclose his name address, and other information cannot be the basis of an arrest. <u>State v. White</u>, 97 Wn.2d 92, at 103, 640 P.2d 1061 (1982).

Indeed, there is no general requirement in this country for citizens to carry any identification. <u>State v. Barwick</u>, 66 Wn. App. 706 at 709, 833 P.2d 421 (July 30, 1992).

We must emphasize that we do not hold that a suspect may be detained and searched merely because he either refused to identify himself or refused to produce proof of identification. Nor do we hold that each time an officer conducts a Terry stop he may immediately conduct a search for identification. People v. Loudermilk, 241 Cal.Rptr. 208 (1987)

Police power is the exercise of the sovereign right of a government to promote order, safety, health, morals, and the general welfare of society, within constitutional limits. Marshall v. Kansas City, Mo. 35 sw 2nd, p 877. (1962).

As a rule, fundamental limitations of regulations under the police power are found in the spirit of the constitution, not in its letter; but they are just as efficient as if expressed in the clearest language Mehlos v. Milwaukee, 146 NW 882 (1914).

A license fee is a charge made primarily for regulation, with the fee to cover costs and expenses of supervision or regulation State v. Jackson, 60 Wisc.2d 700; 211 NW.2d 480 at 487 (1973).

The permission, by competent authority to do an act which without permission, would be illegal, a trespass, or a tort. People v. Henderson, 218 NW.2d 2 at 4 (1974).

Appendix 3: Further Readings

- Carl Miller, *Know Your Constitution* (VHS)

- Frédéric Bastiat, *The Law*

- Henry Hazlitt, *Economics In One Lesson*

- Marc Stevens, *Adventures In Legal Land*

- Murray Rothbard, *For a New Liberty: The Libertarian Manifesto*

- *The Federaist Papers*

- *The Anti-Federalist Papers*

- Robert F. Utter, Hugh D. Spitzer, *The Washington State Constitution* 2nd ed.

Made in the USA
San Bernardino, CA
01 February 2018